Thirsting Soul

Thirsting Soul

The saving work of God
in the heart of man

Roger Fellows

EP

EVANGELICAL PRESS

EVANGELICAL PRESS
Faverdale North Industrial Estate, Darlington, DL3 0PH, England

Evangelical Press USA
P. O. Box 84, Auburn, MA 01501, USA

e-mail: sales@evangelicalpress.org

web: www.evangelicalpress.org

First published 2002

British Library Cataloguing in Publication Data available

ISBN 0 85234 506 2

Printed and bound in Great Britain by
Creative Print and Design Wales
Ebbw Vale
Gwent
NP3 5SD

Dedication

To my wife Pamela who has been a tremendous encouragement throughout my ministry, and has been a great help in making suggestions about this book.

Contents

Introduction

Most news is not good these days. Just pick up a newspaper or turn on the radio or the T.V. You don't have to read, listen or watch the news for long without being bombarded with accounts of war, terrorism, crime, famine, economic chaos and political or even royal scandals. If someone had news that was consistently good you would think that people would flock to hear it. The gospel is good news: that is what the word 'gospel' means. It is the good news that Jesus commanded his disciples to proclaim all over the world (Matt. 28:18-20). It is the good news that has been proclaimed from pulpits, platforms and across tables and fences for two thousand years. Today it is being beamed around the world by radio and television, and reaching more geographical territory than ever before. But is the gospel welcomed as good news? Some would tell us that more people are accepting the gospel than ever before, and that is possible because the population of the world is increasing at such a rate. The fact remains that most people do not look upon the gospel as good news. The vast majority of the human race has no interest in the gospel. That may seem incredible, but it is true. The gospel brings the best possible news for mankind, but they do not want it.

We will see the reason for this as we proceed, but for now we should find out exactly what the gospel is. How do we define it? This can be done in many ways. We could see the letter to the Romans as a full development of the gospel. Paul declares his eagerness to preach the gospel to those at Rome (chapter 1:15), and then goes on to expound the gospel through the epistle as he unfolds God's great plan of salvation.

Paul also gives what could be viewed as a summary of the gospel in his first letter to the Corinthians. After speaking about the gospel that was preached to them and was the means of their salvation, he defines it as follows: ... 'That Christ died for our sins according to the Scriptures, that he was buried, that he was raised on the third day according to the Scriptures...' (I Cor. 15:3,4).

We could perhaps reduce this even further to the simple statement, 'God saves sinners.' The gospel is about a plan of salvation; a plan that only God could conceive and carry out. It is also a plan that was formulated for those who could not save themselves – sinners. Hence, God saves sinners.

In this book we shall endeavour to develop this theme. Where is the appropriate starting point of the gospel? It is tempting to start right at the good news itself, but that is not where the Bible usually starts. For example, in the book of Romans, Paul declares his intention to unfold the gospel, but for about two chapters he speaks of sin and judgement. He doesn't get to the good news itself until the middle of chapter three. Mark begins his book, which we call his Gospel, with these words: 'The beginning of the gospel about Jesus Christ, the Son of God' (Mark 1:1).

Mark then proceeds, not immediately with good news, but with an account of the ministry of John the Baptist, which is essentially a call to repentance. Later in the chapter Mark describes how Jesus began to preach the gospel (verse 14): 'The time has come,' he said. 'The kingdom of God is near. Repent and believe the good news' (Mark 1:15).

What it comes down to is this: the good news begins with bad news. The wonderful description of God's work of salvation is preceded by a dismal account of man's wickedness. Such an approach is not unusual. We are accustomed to a mixture of good and bad news. The doctor may say; 'I can cure your problem, but it will require surgery.' The mechanic may put it this way; 'I'll soon have your car purring like a kitten, but it will cost you £1000.' It is considered good psychology to put the good news first to cushion the blow that the bad news will bring. However, with God's good news he chooses to give us the bad news first. Why does he do this? The answer is simple: unless we accept the bad news, we are not ready for the good news. Unless people are convinced that they are sinners they will not seek a Saviour. Jesus said: '...It is not the healthy who need a doctor, but the sick. I have not come to call the righteous but sinners to repentance' (Luke 5:31,32).

Jesus did not mean that there were people so righteous that they did not need his message; rather he was referring to the Pharisees who thought they were righteous. Some awareness of sin and need was necessary before people would seek help from the Lord. We cannot demand any particular time or level of conviction before pointing people to Christ, but the words of Jesus are a clear statement of the fact that without some sense of sin, people will not seek salvation. The very word 'salvation' implies deliverance from some danger. If there is no danger seen, then no help will be sought. The swimmer proceeding strongly across the lake does not cry out 'Help! Save me'. Nor does the person who gets all his or her thrills in this world or the self-righteous person who seems to have their life in order, 'cry out for help'.

We believe therefore that the appropriate and scriptural starting place for the gospel is the doctrine of sin. People must first be shown their true condition in God's sight before they will seek to know God's remedy for sin.

As we develop these studies we will begin with the human race; their sin and need. From there we will trace God's salvation from the planning stage in eternity past to the completion of it in glory.

1

What is Man? – Depravity

If the gospel can be defined very briefly as 'God saves sinners,' then we need to ask ourselves: 'Where does man come in? What part do we play in our salvation?' Obviously God does the main part, but is man just passive? How big a part does he play? Of course we include women and children in that word for the human race. Is man like a person totally paralysed who must be helped even to eat? Or is he like someone wanting to enter a palace, the door is opened, and he simply walks in? It all depends how much ability man has – whatever man cannot do, God can do. But how much can man do? Our understanding of the gospel and God's work in salvation will be profoundly influenced by our view of man. We must be right at this point or our views of the gospel will be defective. So what is man? What is the condition of the human race? Perhaps the first thing to realize is that man has not always been the same. We do not start off in life as Adam and Eve began. Actually human nature can be viewed in four states:

- 1. **Innocence** – as Adam and Eve were created in the Garden of Eden.
- 2. **Depravity** – the state in which all are born since the sinful fall of Adam and Eve.
- 3. **Grace** – the state of all who are Christians in this life.

- **4. The eternal state** – which can be further divided into
  (a) Glory – the eternal condition of true Christians.
  (b) Everlasting torment – the eternal condition of unbelievers.

Adam and Eve were originally created without sin. They were made in God's image or likeness. They were like God in many ways and enjoyed fellowship with him. Things soon changed, however, for sin came in and spoiled God's perfect creation. The effects of what we call 'the Fall' were numerous and several are listed in Genesis 3. There is an ongoing warfare between Satan and the human race. Childbirth is accompanied by pain and sorrow. The ground is cursed with thorns and weeds. Work has become painful and sweat-producing. We know also that sickness and death began with the Fall. Worse still, man was cast out of the Garden of Eden and cut off from fellowship with God. Instead of sweet communion with God, man now faces his wrath (Rom. 1:18). This is a condition of spiritual death (Eph. 2: 1).

Humanity is sinful

In answer to the question, 'What is man?', we answer first that man is sinful. If anyone asks, 'What is sin?', we say that it is any behaviour contrary to the will of God. Romans 3:23 is a familiar verse: 'For all have sinned and fall short of the glory of God.'

The second part of the verse could be viewed as an explanation of the first part: to sin is to fall short of the glory of God. It is to be ungodlike. It is to disobey God's commands. John defines sin as 'lawlessness' (1 John 3:4). That means that sin is always to be measured in terms of God's commands. God wants us to be like himself. That being so, his moral commands are a reflection of his own character, and to break those commands is to sin against him.

We are all sinners, as the above verse indicates. There are numerous passages in the Bible that tell us we are all sinners, and therefore all are guilty before God. We are not only guilty of breaking God's commands, but we are also guilty of failing to fulfil his commands. Solomon puts it well: 'There is not a righteous man on earth who does what is right and never sins' (Eccles. 7:20).

Sin is not only to be seen as acts of sin, but as our very nature. What makes us sinners? Is it our sinful acts or words? No! We are sinners not just because we sin but because we have sinful natures. Does its barking make a dog a dog? No! A dog is a dog whether or not it barks. In fact it barks because it is a dog. Likewise it is not sinning that makes us sinners, but rather we sin because we are sinners. That is our nature: we were born sinners. From birth we had a tendency to sin. Any parent knows that you do not have to teach a child to sin; it is natural. That is all part of what we call the Fall. The whole human race is sinful.

Humanity is helpless

Not only are we sinners but we are utterly unable to please God by ourselves. As Paul writes: 'Those controlled by the sinful nature cannot please God' (Rom. 8:8). Our nature is now depraved. What does that mean? Theologians often use the expression 'total depravity' to refer to the human condition. But what does it mean? We might say that a glass is totally filled with water. In that case there would be no room for any more. But that doesn't apply to man. However bad he is, he can always be worse. The totality is not in the degree of depravity but in the extent. Man is depraved through and through. His mind is depraved. This is aptly expressed in Genesis 6:5: 'The LORD saw how great man's wickedness on the earth had become, and that every inclination of the thoughts of his heart was only evil all the time.'

His thinking is warped and self-centred with no room for God (Ps. 10:4). His emotions are depraved – he seeks to gratify his natural desires to his own satisfaction. His will is also depraved – every decision he makes is governed by his own selfish ends. Even his body is affected by sin, and he often uses it for purposes that are dishonouring to God. In Romans 2, Paul has a long list of quotations from the Old Testament showing how sin has affected the throat, the tongue, the lips, the mouth, the feet and the eyes (Rom. 2:13-18).

Of particular importance, in view of our consideration of the gospel, is man's inability – not what he can do, but what he cannot. Man may do many things that are good from a human point of view. He may even do certain things that outwardly conform to what God commands, but his motives are always selfish, or at best for the benefit of other people. Nothing he does can please God or in any way merit God's favour. Notice the following descriptions of man's spiritual condition. Jesus in addressing the Jews said: 'Why is my language not clear to you? Because you are unable to hear what I say' (John 8:43).

Paul wrote: 'The god of this age has blinded the minds of unbelievers, so that they cannot see the light of the gospel of the glory of Christ, who is the image of God (2 Cor. 4:4). 'The man without the Spirit does not accept the things that come from the Spirit of God, for they are foolishness to him, and he cannot understand them, because they are spiritually discerned' (I Cor. 2:14). 'As for you, you were dead in your transgression and sins' (Eph. 2:1).

Man is deaf, blind, and ignorant: in fact he is dead. What can he do then to make himself a Christian? It is not surprising that Jesus said: 'No one can come to me unless the Father who sent me draws him, ...' (John 6:44, see also verse 65). Man sounds pretty helpless doesn't he? Rather like the paralysed person who can do nothing without help.

Someone will doubtless ask, 'What about free will? Doesn't man have the ability to choose to follow Christ if he wants to?' It certainly doesn't sound like it from the passages we have quoted. But it is helpful to distinguish between free agency and free will. Of course we have a will: we make decisions all day long. In most cases we can do what we want. We are not normally forced to do things by constraint. We act freely. Certainly God does not make us act against our will, so in this sense we are free agents. But are we free to do what we want? Everyone must admit that there are times when we will to do something but cannot. We may be hindered by stature, weakness, sickness or circumstances. How many of us have been determined to win a race or lift a certain object only to be denied? We have willed to arrive at some destination only to be prevented by an accident.

In the moral realm our inability to do what we want is even more pronounced. How many have willed to give up drinking, smoking, drugs or some other enslaving habit or sinful practice, yet have found themselves unable to do so? This just confirms the passage quoted earlier: '...The sinful mind is hostile to God. It does not submit to God's law, nor can it do so. Those controlled by the sinful nature cannot please God' (Rom. 8:7,8).

Especially relevant to our subject is man's inability with regard to the gospel. He cannot of himself exercise faith in Christ. We have already quoted the words of Jesus: 'No one can come to me unless the Father who sent me draws him, ... (John 6:44). We have already stated that because we are spiritually blind, deaf, ignorant and in fact dead, we are therefore utterly helpless and cannot turn to the Lord. We cannot forsake our sins. We cannot trust in Christ. We cannot even understand the gospel without divine help. The controlling factor is our nature.

Consider the following verse: 'Can the Ethiopian change his skin or the leopard its spots? Neither can you do good who are accustomed to doing evil' (Jer. 13:23).

A black man might paint his skin white but that wouldn't make him a white man. You could paint a leopard with black and white stripes, but that wouldn't make it a zebra. You might make it look very much like a zebra, but the test would come when you fed it. Given the choice of meat or hay which will it choose? Of course it will choose the meat – every time. Its nature determines that. You could say that the leopard has free will to choose the hay, but it is controlled by its nature and therefore it will always choose the meat, whatever colour its coat has been painted. Likewise you could say that the sinner has free will to choose to do good or to believe in Christ, but he is controlled by his nature – his sinful nature, so he will choose to carry on in his sin – every time. For the leopard to choose the hay it would need a change of nature; and for the sinner to choose Christ as his Lord and Saviour, he would need a change of nature – a new birth. So much for free will!

So when anyone is saved it is not because he has chosen Christ, although he may be conscious of doing that. The underlying reason is that God has worked in his heart to make him willing to choose Christ. God grants repentance: that is, he enables people to turn away from their sins. When the Jews heard that Gentiles had been converted, they said, after their initial prejudice had been overcome: '...So then, God has even granted the Gentiles repentance unto life' (Acts 11:18).

'No one can turn from sin unless God enables them to do so. Likewise with faith. Paul reminded the Ephesians: 'For it is by grace you have been saved, through faith – and this not from yourselves, it is the gift of God –' (Eph. 2:8). We cannot and we will not believe unless God gives us faith. In the Word of God, salvation is consistently said to be the work of God. John, after describing the rejection of Christ by the world at large and by the Jews in particular, speaks of those who do accept him: 'Yet to all who received him, to those who believed in his name, he gave the right to become children of God – children born not of natural descent, nor of human decision or a husband's will, but born of God' (John 1:12, 13). Paul speaks in a similar vein about salvation: 'It does not, therefore, depend on man's desire or effort, but on God's mercy (Rom. 9:16).

Someone may ask, 'How can man be held responsible for things he cannot do?' If it is impossible for people to turn to Christ, how can they be punished for not being Christians? You might think it is like telling a child to fly, and then spanking him for not doing it. But the parallel is not good. A child was never intended to fly, and is in no way responsible for that inability. A better analogy is that of a drunk driver who kills someone and pleads that he did not know what he was doing. Of course the proper response is that he was responsible for getting himself in that state. And that is true of the sinner. We are responsible for our sinful condition.

In the first three chapters of the Bible we have the account of Adam's disobedience to God. In the Garden of Eden, Adam was on probation, and not just for himself, but for the whole human race. He could be viewed as an ambassador, being the best possible representative that could be found, or, he could be viewed as the seminal head of the race, all mankind being unborn in him. The writer to the Hebrews uses this argument with respect to Levi being unborn in Abraham when he offered tithes to Melchizedek. (see Heb. 7:4-10). Either way we are all involved in the Fall. In Romans 5, Paul discusses the effects of Christ's work and compares and contrasts it with Adam's sin. Both have a profound influence on the entire race for we are all either '*in*' Christ or '*in*' Adam. Adam's sin brought condemnation to his people – that is to the whole race, whereas Christ's work brought blessing and salvation for his people – those of the whole race he has redeemed. There is a parallel throughout. If there is justice in Christ's righteousness being imputed to his people, then there is justice in Adam's sin being imputed to his people. It is probable, according to commentators like John Murray, that when Paul says at the end of verse 12, *'because all sinned'* he means that all sinned in Adam. It is certain from what he says in verse 19 that we were all made or constituted sinners by Adam's sin.

It follows then that the sinful nature with which we are born (Ps. 51:5), and the consequent inability to do good, to please God or to accept Christ, is a just result of Adam's sin. Men are required to keep God's commandments and will be punished for not doing so, even though they cannot cannot keep them. In the same way all men are commanded to repent and believe the gospel, and will be punished for their unbelief even though response is impossible by nature. We may have trouble following the logic of this, but we cannot doubt that God being a just and perfect God will always do what is fair. We heartily concur with Abraham's statement: '...Will not the Judge of all the earth do right?' (Gen. 18:25).

One other question that may be asked is, 'If no one can turn to Christ of themselves, why is the gospel to be offered to people indiscriminately?' Indeed, the gospel is to be preached to 'all creation' (Mark 16:15). One might argue that this is to leave men without excuse. The gospel has been preached to multitudes who reject it, and will be judged for it. The fact remains however that people are without excuse anyway, whether they hear the gospel or not. The main reason is that the preaching or the propagation of the gospel is the means of reaching those whom God does save. 'For since in the wisdom of God the world through its wisdom did not know him, God was pleased through the foolishness of what was preached to save those who believe' (I Cor. 1:21).

God is sovereign in salvation, but he chooses to use means to bring people to himself – invariably, the gospel. Often it is preached, but there are times when he uses a personal testimony, a radio broadcast or the Word of God in written form – the Scriptures or a book or tract.

We do not know who will be saved, and it is not our business to reason that because people cannot turn to the Lord of themselves, there is no point in trying to reach them with the gospel. We are told to proclaim the gospel to all nations, and we know that some will be saved. We must be faithful and leave the results to the Lord.

Man is indeed in a pitiful plight. Fallen, sinful, under the wrath and condemnation of God. Moreover, he can do nothing to help himself. If that were the sum total of the Bible's message there would be no hope for mankind, but praise God, the Bible does not end there. There is a gospel: there is good news. God saves sinners. He does it sovereignly, but he does it wonderfully, though on his terms. If we first see what man is and can do, or rather cannot do, then we are ready to see what God can and will do for sinners.

Homework

- 1. Give a brief description of the gospel
- 2. What are the four states of human nature?
- 3. What were the effects of the Fall?
- 4. What is the difference between people being sinners by practice and sinners by nature?
- 5. What do we mean by total depravity?
- 6. What figures are used in the Bible to portray people's spiritual state, particularly in relation to their ability to receive the gospel?
- 7. If we are unable to keep God's command ments, how can we be held responsible?
- 8. If people cannot respond to the gospel, why bother offering the gospel to them?

2

Making Plans – Election

In considering how God saves sinners, it is helpful to see salvation as a trinitarian work. We believe in one God, but he has revealed himself to be a triune God, that is, he exists in three persons: the Father, the Son and the Holy Spirit. This is not the place to define or defend the doctrine of the Trinity. It is a mystery that our puny minds cannot fully grasp, certainly not in this life. However it is clear that the three divine persons are not identical and that they are distinct in their activities. For example, the Father did not die on the cross; the Son did. It was not the Son who was poured out on the church at Pentecost; it was the Holy Spirit. The three persons work together in perfect harmony, but each has his own particular areas of activity. Abraham Kuyper has written:

> In every work effected by the Father Son and Spirit in common, the power to bring forth proceeds from the Father, the power to arrange from the Son and the power to perfect from the Holy Spirit. (*The Work of the Holy Spirit,*)

Applying this principle to the work of salvation, we see that the planning of salvation belongs to the Father, the execution or procuring of salvation belongs to the Son and the application of it to human hearts belongs to the Holy Spirit.

When we examine election we are in the planning department. It shouldn't surprise us that God plans things. We do not regard disorganization as an admirable trait, and we surely cannot conceive of a God who did not plan all that he did. The alternative to planning is to act on the spur of the moment or by any whim or fancy. God is not like that. God is a sovereign God, that is, he does whatever he wants. But he also plans what he does; this doctrine we call predestination. Note the following Scriptures: 'All the peoples of the earth are regarded as nothing. He does as he pleases with the powers of heaven and the peoples of the earth. No one can hold back his hand or say to him: "What have you done?"' (Dan. 4:35). Those were the words of a heathen king, Nebuchadnezzar, after being humbled by the Lord. Speaking of God, Paul writes: 'For from him and through him and to him are all things. To him be the glory forever!' (Rom. 11:36). Paul is saying that God is the originator or planner of all things. He causes all things to happen, and all things are for him, that is, for his glory. Nothing happens without God. From wars or earthquakes to the death of a sparrow (Matt. 10:29), God is in control of everything.

People often get a distorted view of predestination, so it may be as well to add a few comments about this truth. We could call them safeguards:

A ***first*** safeguard is that it does not make God the author of sin. Being perfect, God cannot sin. He hates it, yet he permits it, and even uses it for his own purpose and glory. The cross is a good example of this. Judas, the Jewish leaders and Pilate were all acting according to the wickedness of their hearts, yet they were fulfilling God's purposes when they caused Jesus' death. Speaking on the day of Pentecost about Jesus, Peter said: 'This man was handed over to you by God's set purpose and foreknowledge; and you, with the help of wicked men, put him to death by nailing him to the cross' (Acts 2:23).

Those Peter addressed shared in the guilt of Jesus' death

with their leaders. A terrible crime had been committed for which they were all accountable, yet when they had done their worst, they had only carried out the will of God. Exactly the same truth is stated in Acts 4:27,28, where the disciples are praying following further threats against them by the Jewish leaders: 'Indeed Herod and Pontius Pilate met together with the Gentiles and the people of Israel in this city to conspire against your holy servant Jesus, whom you anointed. They did what your power and will had decided beforehand should happen.' God is sovereign, yet at the same time man is fully responsible for his actions. God is never the author of sin.

A ***second*** safeguard against a false view of God's absolute sovereignty is a natural consequence of the first – man is never forced by God to act against his will. As we saw in the first chapter, man's will is restricted by his own sinful nature, but he is a free agent. That is why he is responsible for his actions. Judas, Herod and Pilate were not puppets with regard to the death of Jesus.

The ***third*** safeguard is that God's sovereignty does not mean that he always acts directly in causing things to happen. Frequently he uses others to carry out his will. As we have seen, he used Judas and others to bring about the crucifixion. He used heathen kings to punish his people. He called the king of Assyria '...the rod of my anger...' (Isa. 10:5), even though the king thought he was simply extending his own empire in conquering Israel (verse 7). The Lord even uses the devil to work out his own purposes, as is seen very clearly in the book of Job. God said to Satan, '...He [Job] is in your hands...' (Job 2:6), yet in the last chapter we read of the trouble '...the Lord had brought upon him...' (chapter 42:11).

Now if God is sovereign in all things, it would be very strange if salvation were excluded from his control. Election is simply the application of predestination to salvation. Augustus Strong, in his *Systematic Theology* defines election as follows:

> Election is that eternal act of God, by which in his sovereign pleasure, and on account of no foreseen merit in them, he chooses certain out of the number of sinful men to be the recipients of the special grace of his Spirit, and so to be made voluntary partakers of Christ's salvation.

Let us look at this definition piece by piece.

• **1. Election is an eternal act, or decree.** God did not decide in time that certain people should be saved. The choice was made in eternity. Paul says: 'For he chose us in him [Christ] before the creation of the world …' (Eph. 1:4).

• **2. God's choice was made according to his sovereign pleasure, and not because of anything good he saw in us.** Continuing the passage above, the apostle says: '… In love he predestined us to be adopted as his sons through Jesus Christ, in accordance with his pleasure and will –' (Eph. 1:4,5)

• **3. There is nothing in man to cause God to choose anyone.** No one is good enough to be chosen. It is all of His mercy.

• **4. God's choice is made from among sinners.** This is important to see. One of the objections often made about the doctrine of election is that it is unfair. Particularly that it is unfair to those not chosen. The assumption is made that there are many who would like to be saved, but because they are not chosen, they have no chance to be saved. But this is a complete misunderstanding of the truth. God is not dealing with people who want to be saved, but with those who, without exception have rebelled against him and are his enemies. The psalmist paints a vivid picture of the Lord searching for any who would seek after him: 'The Lord looks down from heaven on the sons of men to see if there are any who understand, any who seek God' (Ps. 14:2). The result of his search is given in the following verse: 'All have turned aside, they have together become corrupt; there is no one who does good, not even one' (verse 3). Paul quotes this with a slight change: 'There is no one … who seeks God' (Rom 3:11).

So when God chooses people to be saved, he is choosing those who, left to themselves, would never even want to be saved – it is totally of grace. And as for those who are not chosen, they are simply being left to do exactly what they want to do – go on in their sin. If any are saved, it is only by grace: and if any are lost, it is their own fault. Can God be criticized for leaving people to do what they want to do?

• **5. People are made voluntary partakers of salvation.** Another point to note in Strong's definition is that no one is forced to accept salvation against their will. All who choose Christ do so willingly and joyfully. Let us quote two more Scripture passages that speak of election: 'Praise be to the God and Father of our Lord Jesus Christ, who has blessed us in the heavenly realms with every spiritual blessing in Christ. For he chose us in him before the creation of the world to be holy and blameless in his sight. In love he predestined us to be adopted as his sons through Jesus Christ, in accordance with his pleasure and will –' (Eph. 1:3-5). 'But we ought always to thank God for you, brothers loved by the Lord, because from the beginning God chose you to be saved through the sanctifying work of the Spirit and through belief of the truth' (2 Thess. 2:13). Both of these passages speak clearly of God choosing (electing) people for salvation and its blessings.

No one can deny that there is a biblical doctrine of election. However, not everyone agrees as to what the doctrine teaches. Let us examine some of the objections made against the doctrine as we have stated it, and in answering them we will develop the theme a little further. The first two may be dismissed fairly quickly.

There are those who contend that election only applies to the Jews as a nation, and has no reference to individuals.

Certainly Israel as a nation were chosen by God out of all other nations (Deuteronomy 7:6), but in the New Testament, election is personal and not limited to Jews. The two passages just quoted come from epistles that were addressed primarily to Gentile converts: '...Formerly you who are Gentiles by birth...' (Eph. 2:11). '...You suffered from your own countrymen the same things those churches suffered from the Jews,' (1 Thess. 2:14).

Another view of election is that it is election to privilege or service, but not to salvation. That is hard to accept in view of the clear statement in 2 Thessalonians 2:13 that God has chosen us to be 'saved'.

A view that is commonly held is that election is personal, and it is for salvation, but there is no arbitrary choice, for God looked ahead in time, saw those who would believe, and therefore chose them. The keystone of this view is the use of the word 'foreknow', as for example in Rom. 8:29: 'For those God foreknew he also predestined...' The teaching presumes that 'foreknew' means simply that God knew ahead of time what these people would do. However, there are some serious problems with this view.

First: the word 'know' itself often means far more than intellectual awareness. This is true throughout the Bible. For example, in Genesis 4:1 we read that 'Adam lay with his wife', referring obviously to a sexual act. The word 'lay' is really 'knew', and is translated as such in the King James Version of the Bible (KJV). In Amos 3:2, God said of Israel: 'You only have I chosen of all the families of the earth...' Once again the word 'chosen' is really 'known' as in the KJV. Clearly God knows all families (nations) on earth, but the knowledge referred to here is intimate knowledge. It is the knowledge of love and sovereign choice.

In Matthew 7:23 the Lord tells his hearers that at the day of judgement some will hear the dreadful words from his lips,

'… I never knew you. Away from me…' It is the all-knowing judge of men who speaks. He knew every thought that ever passed through their minds, but in the sense of an intimate, loving relationship, the Lord did not know them. We believe then that just as knowledge is often used in the sense of intimate knowledge, so foreknowledge usually refers to God's purposing ahead of time to bring people into a loving relationship with himself.

Second: that the words 'foreknow' or 'foreknowledge' are used in this way is clear from other scriptural passages. Speaking to the Jews about the Lord Jesus Christ, Peter said: 'This man was handed over to you by God's set purpose and foreknowledge; and you, with the help of wicked men, put him to death by nailing him to the cross' (Acts 2:23). That God knew in advance that Jesus would be crucified, goes without saying, but the point of Peter's statement is surely that Jesus' death was planned by God. The word implies sovereign determination ahead of time.

The same is true of another passage in Peter's letter. He is speaking again of the death of Jesus: 'He was chosen before the creation of the world' (1 Peter 1:20). The word 'chosen' is 'foreknown', the same basic word we have been considering. God did not only know that Jesus would die, he chose and ordained that Jesus would die. So when Paul says in Romans 8:29 that God 'foreknew' his people, he means far more than that he knew ahead of time what they would do. He foreknew his people with a sovereign love. He determined to do them good. He determined to make them his people.

Third: another fatal objection to foreknowledge being only knowledge of future events is that this would remove all sovereignty from God. His choice of people for salvation would simply rest on their choice of Christ. He saw that when given the opportunity to believe, they would do so, and therefore he chose them. To say the least, this is illogical. It is not too much to say that it is also an insult to the Almighty. His hands are tied. He can only choose people if they will first choose him!

Fourth: such a view of election is quite contrary to many biblical passages. Let me quote a selection. 'Yet to all who received him, to those who believed in his name, he gave the right to become children of God – children born not of natural descent, nor of human decision or a husband's will, but born of God' (John 1:12,13). Faith in Christ brings us into God's family, but it is a divine operation and not the result of a human decision. 'What then shall we say? Is God unjust? Not at all! For he says to Moses, "I will have mercy on whom I have mercy, and I will have compassion on whom I have compassion." It does not therefore, depend on man's desire or effort, but on God's mercy. For the Scripture says to Pharaoh: "I raised you up for this very purpose, that I might display my power in you, and that my name might be proclaimed in all the earth." Therefore God has mercy on whom he wants to have mercy, and he hardens whom he wants to harden' (Rom. 9:14-18). Nothing could be plainer in this passage than that God sovereignly chooses whom he wants to save. 'Brothers, think of what you were when you were called. Not many of you were wise by human standards; not many were influential; not many were of noble birth. But God chose the foolish things of the world to shame the wise: God chose the weak things of the world to shame the strong. He chose the lowly things of this world and the despised things – and the things that are not – to nullify the things that are, so that no one may boast before him' (I Cor. 1:26-29).

If salvation depended on man's choice, then he would have some grounds for boasting that he was smart enough to figure out the gospel, and to accept it, but God has determined that this will not happen. Not only does he decide who will be saved, but he has designed things so that in general people who are less than brilliant, with no standing in this world, are chosen or called (we will explain the meaning of 'called' later). In this way God gets all the glory. The fact is, that if God did not choose us, we would never be saved, for as we saw in the first chapter, no one can or will choose Christ of themselves. Left to ourselves we would all perish.

Why is it that some Christians are afraid of the doctrine of election? Indeed, some are downright hostile towards it. Perhaps the most basic reason is that people like to think that they are in charge of their own destiny. Inherent in all of us is the attitude expressed in the lines of a poem by William Ernest Henley: 'I am the master of my fate; I am the captain of my soul.' We like to feel that we can have the final say in such an important matter as salvation. If God has the last word, then it makes us less significant. But as we have already pointed out, if the choice were left to us, it would always be '*No*'. We would invariably say, 'We don't want this man to be our king.' One thing required of a believer is humility. That begins when we realize that we don't deserve salvation, nor would we seek it of ourselves

Some may be thinking that I have gone too far in playing down human choice. After all, don't we make a choice to become Christians? Yes we do, and doubtless many genuine believers think that they had the last word in deciding to follow Christ. That is unfortunate and completely wrong, and it is in many cases the result of teaching they received at the time they became Christians. When anyone makes a decision to become a Christian it is only because the Lord has brought them to that place. Jesus said, 'No one can come to me unless the Father who sent me draws him...' (John 6:44). It follows therefore that everyone who does come to Christ has first been drawn by the Father. His or her decision to trust the Saviour and follow him comes as a result of a prior work of the Lord in their heart. More of this later.

There are other reasons why election, as we have defined it, is an unpopular doctrine. We have already dealt with the accusation that it is unfair. I would just add the question; would we rather God dealt with us fairly, or mercifully? If we all received our just deserts we would have no hope whatever. Mercy is our only hope, and if we are Christians, it is because we have received mercy. It would be better to focus on the wonder of election rather than on its supposed limitations. What amazing grace that each believer was chosen by God before the world began to be his child! How this truth should thrill us and encourage us!

Some would say that the doctrine of election discourages the unconverted; that is, it makes them feel there is no point in trying to become a Christian if they do not know they are elect; but I have not found that to be so. When the doctrine of election was widely taught, and even taught in an unbalanced way so as to ignore human responsibility, some may have been discouraged by it, but such a thing is almost unheard of in these days. Every objection I have heard against the doctrine has come from those who profess to believe in Christ.

Another objection against this truth is that it discourages evangelism. Those who hold to the doctrine of election are supposed to believe that if God has determined to save certain people, then it doesn't matter whether or not they hear the gospel for they will be saved anyway. But this is a complete distortion of the truth. God has not only decided who will be saved, but also the means for their salvation, and that invariably involves taking the gospel to them. Jesus told his disciples to preach the gospel to '...all creation...' (Mark 16:15). Anyone who makes the doctrine of election an excuse for not spreading the gospel to every nation is being disobedient to the Lord. We have to admit there have been some who have followed that line of thinking; we refer to them as 'hypercalvinists'. On the other hand there have been many who have held firmly to the doctrine of election and have had a burning zeal for the conversion of the lost. This would include the reformers – Luther,

Zwingle, Knox and many more; great evangelists like Whitefield and Spurgeon; also pioneer missionaries such as John Eliot and William Carey.

When Paul was in Corinth he seemed discouraged because of the opposition, but the Lord encouraged him in a vision, saying to him: '... Do not be afraid; keep on speaking, do not be silent. For I am with you, and no one is going to attack and harm you, because I have many people in this city' (Acts 18:9,10). The apostle had already seen some people converted to the Lord under his ministry, but the Lord assured him that there would be many more. God had his elect people there and they would respond to the gospel. The doctrine of election thus became an encouragement to evangelism.

We may not know exactly when people will respond to the gospel, but we do know that God has his elect people scattered in this world. The gospel is the only means of reaching them, so we know that eventually our work in the Lord is not in vain. (1 Cor. 15:58).

Election is a wonderfully encouraging truth – to think that God set His love upon us from all eternity – but it is also humbling. There was nothing in us to influence God's choice. We are certainly no better than other people. Paul asked the Corinthians, 'For who makes you different from anyone else?...' (1 Cor. 4:7). The answer is of course, only God makes us different. We are not Christians because we are more spiritual or discerning than others. We are not in God's family because we chose to be. We are not heirs of the world to come because of any merit in us. It is all of grace. God chose us because he chose us. He loved us because he wanted to love us, and in some mysterious way he gets glory to himself because of it. We could not make ourselves Christians, we could not even understand the gospel. But God decided to make us his children, and therefore we are. If we cannot fully understand all the ramifications, let us at least rejoice that we are now saved and have eternal life.

Homework

- 1. What do we mean when we say that salvation is a trinitarian work?
- 2. If God predestines everything that happens, is man just a puppet? Why not?
- 3. How would you answer the argument that God's choice of sinners for salvation is based upon his foreseeing that they would accept Christ?
- 4. Can people be saved if they are not elect?
- 5. Is it unfair for God not to choose some people? Why not?
- 6. How can we know if someone is one of the elect?
- 7. Why do we need to evangelize if the elect are sure to be saved?
- 8. Of what value is the doctrine of election to the Christian?

3

Rescued by Death – Atonement

We have seen that despite man's sinful and depraved state, God in his mercy has not left the human race to perish but has planned salvation for sinners. How is this to be accomplished? We saw in the last chapter that salvation is a trinitarian work. Election is the Father's work of planning salvation and choosing those who will be saved. Atonement is the work of God's Son, the Lord Jesus Christ. The English word atonement means reconciliation – 'at-one-ment'. The meaning of the Hebrew word is debated, some arguing for 'covering' (for sin), and others for 'ransom'. In relation to the gospel we use the word to refer to the work of Christ in dealing with sin. Christ provides a way for those chosen by the Father to experience the salvation for which they have been chosen. It is impossible for sinful people to come to a God who is perfectly holy; somehow their sins must be dealt with. That was why Jesus came into this world. Before his birth he was given the name 'Jesus' by the angel: '...give him the name Jesus, because he will save his people from their sins' (Matt. 1:21).

'Jesus' means 'God saves'. His ministry, although many-faceted, was primarily aimed at the salvation of God's people. How was this accomplished? There were many wonderful things about the life of Jesus. He was kind and compassionate (Acts 10:38); he was a teacher without equal (John 7:46); he performed many miracles (Luke 19:37); his life was blameless

(John 8:46). However, the most important thing about Jesus' ministry was not his life but his death, and it is clearly taught in Scripture that in his death Jesus atoned for sin. '...Christ died for our sins according to the Scriptures' (1 Cor. 15:3). 'For Christ died for sins once for all, the righteous for the unrighteous, to bring you to God...' (1 Peter 3:18)

Normally when you read a biography you expect to have something of the person's family history. There will be some reference to his death and perhaps to the honour given to him at his funeral, but the great majority of the book will be taken up with the life and accomplishments of the person. The New Testament has four separate accounts of Jesus' life: the Gospels of Matthew, Mark, Luke and John. What is soon apparent is that each of the four writers give an amazingly large amount of their account to the death of Jesus and the events immediately surrounding it. Actually about one third of the Gospels deal with the period from Jesus' entry into Jerusalem five days before his death, to the time of his ascension. This statistic alone should alert us to the fact that there is something very important about Jesus' death.

In connection with this there are many references in the New Testament to the blood of Christ as being effective in salvation. The shedding of blood refers to death: it is the evidence of death – a violent death. In the Old Testament it was used of the animal sacrifices whose blood was shed before they were offered on the altar. References to Christ's blood show that Jesus is the fulfilment of these sacrifices. It also reminds us that his death was a violent one. Teaching concerning Jesus' blood is widespread: we are *reconciled* by his blood (Eph. 2:13); *redeemed* by his blood (Eph. 1:7, 1 Peter 1:18,19); *justified* by his blood (Rom. 5:9); *cleansed* by his blood (1John 1:7); we have a *sacrifice of atonement* – (or a better word, *propitiation*) through his blood (Rom. 3:25). Some of these are technical terms but it is not possible to avoid such words without losing the sense of what they convey.

Reconciliation is fairly obvious. We were estranged from God. Our sins had separated us from him, but because Christ died and shed his blood, the barrier that barred us from God's presence is removed, and we are reconciled to him.

Redemption means setting free by the payment of a price. A good picture is that of a slave market. Here are people who have been enslaved and are the property of another. Someone comes along, has pity on them, pays the required price and then sets them free. A similar term is ransom, where someone has been abducted and held for ransom until the price demanded has been paid. We had sold ourselves to the devil and were under his control. The Lord Jesus Christ came, had pity on us and paid the price for our freedom: not money, but his own precious blood. We must avoid taking the illustration too far. Some, to be consistent have said that the price was paid to the devil; however, Scripture does not teach that. Christ presented his blood to God as the book of Hebrews shows in speaking of Christ as our High Priest, taking his blood into the Most Holy Place (Heb. 9:7,24,25).

Justification is a legal term. A prisoner is in the dock. The evidence against him is overwhelming – he is clearly guilty. His crimes are worthy of death. Normally he would be condemned and sentenced, but instead he is acquitted – he is justified instead of being condemned. The judge sets him free. How can this be? His crime is forgiven, not because it has been overlooked, but because another has taken the punishment. Jesus has acted as his substitute and been punished in the place of the sinner. If someone argues that our legal system does not allow for one person to take the place of another, we can only answer that an all wise, almighty God has said that he is satisfied with such an arrangement. He justifies the wicked (Romans 4:5), for, at the moment we believe in Jesus Christ we are still in our sins and wicked, but God pardons us and declares us righteous, that is, justified. So we are justified by Christ's blood. We will look more closely at this in a later chapter.

Cleansing is quite obvious in its meaning. In the Old Testament it was often used in a ceremonial sense. In the temple the Jews had to undergo various rites with water to keep themselves and others ceremonially clean. We are cleansed from all sin and defilement through Jesus' shed blood.

Propitiation is not a word in common usage today, and several modern translations of the Bible have tried to substitute better known terms. However this has not usually been helpful. The NIV uses 'sacrifice of atonement' which is certainly a biblical idea, but does not exactly convey what the original word means. Propitiation is appeasement, the turning aside of wrath. 'The wrath of God is being revealed from heaven against all the godlessness and wickedness of men who suppress the truth by their wickedness' (Rom. 1:18).

God is angry with sinners and unless that anger is turned aside from us, we will surely perish. But Christ, in taking our place, has received the full measure of God's wrath against sin, and now God is propitiated, appeased. His anger is turned aside. This only happens because of Jesus' death and shed blood – we have propitiation through faith in his blood.

Christ by his death secures the salvation planned by God from eternity. We have already said enough to indicate why Jesus' death secures salvation. Perhaps it is best summarised in the word 'substitution'. Jesus was our substitute: he took our place. We deserve God's punishment because of our sins, but Christ in his great love bore our sins and took that punishment. '...The Lord has laid on him the iniquity of us all' (Isa. 53:6). 'He himself bore our sins in his body on the tree...' (1 Peter 2:24). Paul puts it even more strikingly: 'God made him who had no sin to be sin for us...' (2 Cor. 5:21).

What an amazing statement! Jesus, who was pure and absolutely without sin, was made sin. Sin was imputed to him. He was treated as if he were nothing but sin. In this state even the Father turned aside from him, bringing forth the awful cry from Jesus: '...My God, my God, why have you forsaken me?' (Matt. 27:46). We can never understand that cry unless we see that Jesus was being a substitute for his people, bearing their sins and taking their punishment.

Although the clearest teaching about Jesus' death is found in the New Testament, the Old Testament lays the foundation for his work. It is not too much to say that we cannot fully comprehend Jesus' work without an understanding of the Old Testament. There were many specific predictions or prophecies of the coming of Jesus the Messiah ('Messiah' is the Hebrew equivalent of the Greek word 'Christ'. It means 'the anointed one' and refers to the promised deliverer the Jews were expecting). There were prophecies about his family (Gen. 49:10, Isa. 11:1); his birthplace (Micah 5:2); his virgin birth (Isa. 7:14); his entry into Jerusalem (Zech. 9:9); and several references to the events occurring at the crucifixion – see particularly Psalms 22 and 69. There are also passages, particularly in Isaiah 53, that show the substitutionary and atoning work of Christ. However we want to look at another aspect of the Old Testament – its typology.

There were many events, ceremonies and objects that pointed forward to the coming of Christ. In particular there was the whole sacrificial system. From the time of Abel, God's people offered animal sacrifices to him. Clearly there were instructions to this effect. It may have been that when God clothed Adam and Eve with animal skins (Gen. 3:21), he was showing them the way of sacrifice for blood had to be shed to get the skins. Certainly Abel knew that God would be pleased with a sacrifice rather than vegetables (Gen. 4:4). Noah offered sacrifices when he came safely out of the ark (Gen. 8:20). Abraham built several altars and the practice was passed on to each succeeding generation. When the tabernacle was built, instructions for sacrifices were given in detailed form, particularly in the early chapters of Leviticus.

But why such a gruesome practice? Why the need for all these deaths and the splashing of blood around the altars? It taught the people that they could not come to God except on the basis of sacrifice. It showed God's hatred of sin. They were sinners and as such were cut off from fellowship with God, but God in his grace provided a way for them to approach him. They could bring an animal sacrifice, lay their hands upon it and kill it. The laying of hands showed their identification with the animal. The one who offered it deserved to die for his sins, but those sins were symbolically transferred to the animal. The animal became a substitute and died instead of the offerer. This was a vivid picture of the coming sacrifice of Jesus at Calvary. When John the Baptist first identified Jesus at the beginning of his public ministry it was in these words: '… Look, the Lamb of God who takes away the sin of the world' (John 1:29).

Jesus was the sacrificial Lamb who was to bear sin, not just for Jews but for those of all nations – the world. The writer to the Hebrews tells us that it was not possible for the blood of animal sacrifices to take away sins (Heb. 10:4). What the animal sacrifices did was to point ahead to Jesus' death on the cross to take away sins.

We see then that the death of Jesus was absolutely essential for sin to be dealt with. On one occasion Jesus was speaking to the disciples about his coming death. Peter could not conceive of Jesus dying and told him so (Matt. 16:22). Jesus' response was sharp: '…Get behind me, Satan!…' (23). Peter's motives were good in trying to shield his beloved Lord from suffering and death, but he did not understand at that point that without Jesus' death there could be no salvation. Jesus' strong words to Peter are a reminder that any attempt to avoid the death of Jesus is satanic. The death of Jesus is crucial for the Christian gospel. When Paul was writing to the church at Corinth he reminds them of his earlier ministry among them: 'For I resolved to know nothing while I was with you except Jesus Christ and him crucified' (1 Cor. 2:2).

Everything Paul preached had its roots in the cross. It was central to his gospel. Without the message of the atonement, that is, salvation through the death and shed blood of Jesus Christ at Calvary, there is no Christian gospel.

The sufficiency of the atonement

Let us look for a moment at the results of Jesus' atoning death. What did his death accomplish?

First: it fully satisfied God's justice. Some people make much of God's love as if that were the only attribute that God possesses. Of course God is love, and his love is marvellous, but God is also holy and just. He never loves at the expense of justice. God has given laws to the human race and these laws demand a system of justice. What point would laws be in our land if they were never upheld? Just think of traffic laws. Speed limits are posted along the roads, but suppose these were never upheld, who would feel safe driving? If laws against burglary, murder and rape were never upheld, what would our society be like? The level of crime is bad enough as it is, but without law enforcement, life would be intolerable.

God, as a just lawgiver, insists that his laws are enforced, and that includes punishing those who break his laws. If we have any doubts about the awful nature of sin, or the severity of God's justice, we need only to see how God punishes sinners – by casting those who are unrepentant into hell. Hell is not a popular doctrine today, yet it is often referred to in the Bible. Here are just three references. The first two are the words of Jesus, and the third is written by Paul. No comment is made on the verses for none is needed: 'And if your eye causes you to sin, pluck it out. It is better for you to enter the kingdom of God with one eye than to have two eyes and be thrown into hell, where "their worm does not die, and the fire is not quenched"' (Mark 11:47,48). '…The rich man also died and was buried. In hell, where he was in torment, he looked up and saw Abraham far away, with Lazarus by his side. So he called to him, "Father Abraham, have pity on me and send Lazarus to dip the tip of his finger in water and cool my tongue, because I am in agony in this fire"'(Luke 16:22-24). 'God is just: He will pay back trouble to those who trouble you and give relief to you who are troubled, and to us as well. This will happen when the Lord Jesus is revealed from heaven in blazing fire with his powerful angels. He will punish those who do not know God and do not obey the gospel of our Lord Jesus. They will be punished with everlasting destruction and shut out from the presence of the Lord and from the majesty of his power on the day he comes to be glorified in his holy people and to be marvelled at among all those who have believed…' (2 Thess. 1:6-10)

In the light of this, any scheme of salvation must be just, that is, it must uphold God's laws. God cannot simply overlook our sins for that would be unjust. The apostle John, who tells us that '…God is love…' (1 John 4:16), also tells us that '…God is light…' (1 John 1:5), that is, holy. Jesus in His atoning work fully satisfied divine justice. The law was upheld and sin punished in full. God is '…just and the one who justifies those who have faith in Jesus' (Rom. 3:26).

Second: Jesus' death fully paid the price of sin. Sin is sometimes viewed as a debt. One version of the Lord's prayer says, 'Forgive us our debts.' We owe God perfect obedience to His commands, but as sinners we cannot give that – we fall short. We are therefore debtors. So how can we ever pay? It is like the man in the parable who owed his master 10,000 talents (Matt. 18:24). That was equivalent to hundreds of years wages and therefore was impossible to repay. There is no way anyone can pay God his due, but Jesus paid the debt for us. He paid what we owed – the death penalty. He also gave to God a life of perfect obedience which we also owed.

As he died, Jesus uttered the words '…It is finished…' (John 19:30). Actually in the Greek it is a single word. Not a groan of defeat – 'I'm done for', 'I've had it', but a cry of triumph and accomplishment – 'finished'; 'mission accomplished!' Listen to the words of Hebrews: 'Day after day every priest stands and performs his religious duties; again and again he offers the same sacrifices, which can never take away sins. But when this priest had offered for all time one sacrifice for sins, he sat down at the right hand of God. Since that time he waits for his enemies to be made his footstool, because by one sacrifice he has made perfect for ever those who are being made holy' (Heb. 10:11-14).

In the Jewish temple there were no seats. The priest's work was never done. As soon as he was finished with one offering there would be others to attend to. But Jesus, when he offered his sacrifice – his own body; sat down. His work was completed. By one sacrifice he had perfectly atoned for the sins of all God's people. This means that nothing can be added to the work of Christ. Our works, our religious activities, even our faith, add nothing to the finished work of the Saviour.

At this point it might be appropriate to say something about the views of the Roman Catholic Church. Their 'communion' service is very different to that of most protestant churches. They call it the 'mass', and they teach that it is more than a memorial of Christ's death. They believe that in the mass, Christ's death is re-enacted and that he is offered again by the priest as a sacrifice for sins. But the verses quoted above from Hebrews 10, and others in the same book, make it very clear than no further sacrifice for sin is needed. Christ has fully paid the price for sin. To teach otherwise is to deny his work (see also Heb. 7:27; 9:12,25,26).

The Church of Rome also teaches that virtually all believers – that is all who are not perfect when they die, must spend some time in a place called purgatory where they will suffer for their sins. Purgatory is said to be a place of unspeakable suffering, the same as hell except that it is not permanent. So believers will suffer in purgatory according to the sins they have committed in this life; for while God forgives sins, his justice still demands that the believer suffer the full payment for his or her sins before they can enter heaven. Some will suffer more and longer than others, but eventually they will leave purgatory and go to heaven, though no one can know for sure how long that will be.

There are several erroneous aspects of this doctrine, but the most serious error is that it implies that Christ's sufferings are not sufficient to atone fully for sin, and the believer must suffer himself to achieve that full atonement. This doctrine is wrong; it has not a shred of biblical support. Christ, as we have seen, offered himself as a sacrifice and sat down – his work being finished. There is no purgatory for believers. All their sins have been paid in full. Hallelujah! This is well expressed in the verse of a hymn:

> Paschal Lamb, by God appointed,
> All our sins on Thee were laid;
> By almighty love anointed,
> Thou hast full atonement made:
> All thy people are forgiven
> Through the virtue of Thy blood;
> Opened is the gate of heaven;
> Peace is made 'twixt man and God.
> *John Bakewell (1721-1819)*

Third: Christ's death accomplished its designed end, that is, the salvation of the elect. Here we must remind ourselves of the truth seen in the previous chapter. God has chosen a people for himself and has given them to his Son. Jesus in turn purchases salvation for those people given to him. There is continuity here. One of the most controversial questions in Christian theology is, 'For whom did Christ die?', or, if you like, 'For which sins did Christ make atonement?' Theoretically there are four possible answers:

- **a.** All the sins of all people
- **b.** All the sins of some people
- **c.** Some of the sins of all people
- **d.** Some of the sins of some people

(John Owen deals with the first three of these more thoroughly in his book *The Death of Death in the Death of Christ.*) The last two can be dismissed together, because if Christ only died for some sins, whether of all or some, then those people still have some sins not paid for. They can never be saved for they must pay for their own sins. We are left then with the first two possibilities.

If the first is true, that Christ died for all the sins of all people, then either all must be saved, or else if they are not, then their sins will be punished twice, first in Christ, then in themselves. It also means that Christ died for some who were already in hell. The position shown in Scripture is that Christ died for all the sins of some people – the elect – those given to him by God. This is in keeping with God's plan of salvation. The doctrine is usually referred to as 'limited atonement' or better, as used in this book, 'particular redemption'.

Scripture teaches it is a biblical doctrine. Note the following passages of Scripture: '... You are to give him the name Jesus, because he will save his people from their sins' (Matt. 1:21). 'This is my blood of the covenant, which is poured out for many...' (Mark 14:24). 'I am the good shepherd. The good shepherd lays down his life for the sheep' (John 10:11). '...Christ loved the church and gave himself up for her' (Eph. 5:25). In all these verses there is a limitation; it is his people he saves, not others. His blood is poured out for many, not all. The shepherd lays down his life for the sheep, not the goats. Christ loved the church as distinct from others.

It has already been shown that such a view of the atonement is in keeping with the whole plan of salvation. If God has planned to save a limited number of sinners, then there would be little purpose in an atonement designed to save all. Again this view is in keeping with the nature of the atonement. We looked earlier at several technical words in connection with Christ's work. For example Christ was a propitiation for sinners. That means that God's wrath is turned away from them. If that is applied to all without exception, then God is no longer angry with anyone – something clearly not true (see Rom. 1:18). Christ has reconciled sinners to God. If all are included, then everyone is reconciled. There is a verse that at first sight seems to teach just that: '...God was reconciling the world to himself in Christ, not counting men's sins against them...' (2 Cor. 5:19). That seems to say that all are reconciled, but note what follows – people's sins are not counted against them – that would be nothing less than justification. It cannot include all without exception, or else all are righteous before God. There is one other relevant verse in the same chapter: 'For Christ's love compels us, because we are convinced that one died for all, and therefore all died' (2 Cor. 5:14).

Once again at first reading it seems to say the opposite of what we have been claiming. It says Christ died for all. But notice there is a consequence – 'therefore'; something happens as a result of his dying for all, and that is that 'all died'. The same people for whom Christ died, also died with him. The New Testament not only teaches that Christ died for his people, but also that they died with him (for example, Rom. 6:2,8; Gal. 2:20). Some maintain that Christ died for all without exception, but very few would teach that all died with Christ, that is, were identified with Him in His death.

We do not pretend that the doctrine of particular redemption (that is that Christ died specifically for his people) is without difficulties. There are a number of objections raised against it, as there are against the doctrine of election. We will look briefly at some of these objections.

First: it limits the work of Christ. Some would even say it limits God's love. Let us be clear that we are not putting any limit upon the work of Christ. If he had died to redeem all, he would not have suffered more. His death is of infinite value, but Scripture teaches, as we have seen, that his death had a particular design.

Whatever view we take of the atonement, it is limited. If we say that Christ died to redeem the whole world, then we have to observe that unless the whole world is saved, things have not worked out as intended, because clearly the whole world will not be saved. As we have seen, there is such a place as hell, and it will be populated. The only way out of that difficulty is to say that Christ died to make it possible for all to be saved. In other words no one's salvation is guaranteed by Christ's death, it is just made possible. There remains the human response of repentance and faith, but as we saw in chapter 1, man's depraved condition leaves him unable of himself to respond anyway.

The Bible does not teach that Christ died to make it possible for people to be saved, but that he died to save his people, his church, his sheep. As Hebrews 9:12 says, Christ '... entered the Most Holy Place... having obtained eternal redemption.' It was not a possibility; it was obtained; it was guaranteed.

Second: another difficulty with the doctrine of particular redemption is that there are a number of Bible verses that seem to teach that Christ died for all. We have already looked at some in 2 Corinthians 5. We could classify the verses as follows:

(a) Those that speak of 'the world', for example: '...Look, the Lamb of God, who takes away the sin of the world! (John

1:29). For God so loved the world that he gave his one and only Son…' (John 3:16).

In the first of these we need to consider language carefully. If the sins of everyone in the world are taken away, then no one need ever fear hell for all must be saved. This cannot be the meaning. John often speaks of the world as distinct from Jews. The Jews thought they had a monopoly on God's grace, but John's message (as well as Jesus' own message) made it clear that there were blessings for Gentiles as well – the world. The same would be true of 1 John 2:2: 'He is the atoning sacrifice [KJV – propitiation] for our sins, and not only for ours but also for the sins of the whole world.' To take this literally would mean, as already observed, that God's anger was turned away from all.

John 3:16 could be taken in the same way, to refer to Gentiles, but it needs to be seen that the emphasis here is not only the object of the love – the world, but the intensity of the love – God ***so*** loved. He so loved the world. Even though the world had consistently rejected God, he loved that world and sent his Son to bring salvation to the world.

This might be an appropriate time to think of God's love in general. When the Bible speaks of God's love, it almost always refers to his redemptive love, whether to the Israelites in the Old Testament or to his New Covenant people. That does not mean, however, that God has no compassion for people in general. Some of the Old Testament prophecies like Jeremiah and Hosea show a God who deeply laments the sins of his people Israel. (e.g. Hosea 11:8). All people are God's creatures. All are the objects of his kind provision. He causes rain and sunshine to fall on the good and the wicked (Matt. 5:45). Moreover although unrepentant sinners will be punished in hell, God has no pleasure in this (Ezek. 18:23). The Lord Jesus Christ wept over the city of Jerusalem for their rejection of him, knowing the judgement that would come upon them. So it cannot be wrong to speak of God's love to all, even though this does not mean that all will be saved.

If someone asks why God does not love people enough to save all, for surely he has the power to do so, it is not easy to give an answer. Indeed, it is impossible to give an adequate answer. He does as he sees fit, and he acts for his own glory. In view of our awful sinfulness and rebellion, the amazing thing is not that some are not saved, but that any are saved. It is all of grace – amazing grace!

(b) A second category of verses that seem to teach that Christ died for all are those verses that use words like 'every' or 'all'. For example: 'But we see Jesus, who was made a little lower than the angels, now crowned with glory and honour because he suffered death, so that by the grace of God he might taste death for everyone' (Heb. 2:9).

If Jesus tasted death for literally everyone, then of course no one will ever need to taste death for themselves. In other words, all will be saved. But we know that is not true. The 'everyone' needs to be interpreted in its context. When Nelson said, 'England expects every man to do his duty,' he obviously meant everyone involved in the battle about to take place – Trafalgar. So the 'everyone' in Hebrews 2:9 must be seen in its context. In the following verse the author speaks of 'bringing many sons to glory'. The 'everyone' for whom Christ tasted death is the same group of 'many sons' he brings to glory.

Another verse often quoted against the limited view of atonement is the following: '...He [the Lord] is patient with you, not wanting anyone to perish, but everyone to come to repentance' (2 Peter 3:9). Some would argue that if God wants all to come to repentance then he must have provided salvation for all. The verse can be approached in one of two ways. If the 'wanting' refers to God's sovereign will, then clearly it is frustrated because not all are saved. In that case it must refer to the elect. Indeed, if God delays the return of Christ (for that is the context) waiting for everyone to be saved, then he will have to wait a long time! It must then refer to those chosen in Christ.

Alternatively, the 'wanting' could simply refer to God's desire for the salvation of people rather than their damnation, something we looked at earlier in the chapter. Another verse that can be viewed in the same light is 1 Timothy 2:4. '...God our Saviour who wants all men to be saved and to come to knowledge of the truth.' It could express God's desire for the salvation of people of all classes (kings etc. – verse 2), or it could refer to a general desire for the salvation of all, without any specific reference to the extent of Christ's atonement.

(c) There is another category of verses that are difficult to interpret in the light of the view we have presented of the atonement. They seem to teach that some for whom Christ died will perish. Now if only one soul for whom Christ died ends up in hell, then the doctrine of particular redemption collapses. Note the following: 'So this weak brother, for whom Christ died, is destroyed by your knowledge' (1 Cor. 8:11). Romans 14:15 is similar.

If the destruction referred to is eternal destruction, then the truth at stake is not just a matter of whether Christ died for the person, but whether a true believer can be lost; something unthinkable in the light of God's saving work. Christ said of his sheep, 'I give them eternal life, and they shall never perish...' (John 10:28). We will examine this in more detail in a later chapter. That being so, then either the situation is hypothetical, that is, Paul is warning of the theoretical danger of causing others to stumble, although he knows it cannot really happen. Nevertheless he gives the warning. More likely, the destruction is some serious damage to the person's life – all sin is destructive.

The most difficult verse of all is 2 Peter 2:1: 'But there were also false prophets among the people, just as there will be false teachers among you. They will secretly introduce destructive heresies, even denying the sovereign Lord who bought them – bringing swift destruction on themselves.'

There is nothing hypothetical or ambiguous here. False teachers will come, and they will perish. The question is, were they really saved? The word 'bought' is usually translated 'redeemed'. If then these teachers were redeemed by the blood of Christ and they perish, the doctrine of particular redemption falls to the ground. The thing to note here is that the word for 'Lord' is not the usual Greek word 'kurios' normally used of the Lord Jesus Christ, but an unusual word 'despotes', from which we get 'despot', an absolute tyrannical ruler. The word is never used in the New Testament of Christ but either of an earthly master, or of God the Father. The buying referred to then in 2 Peter 2:1 must be to something other than Christ's redemption through his shed blood. In the Old Testament, the word 'redemption' was sometimes used to describe deliverance from an unpleasant or dangerous situation. For example it was used of the deliverance of the Israelites from the slavery of Egypt (Deut. 7:8), or of deliverance from cruelty (Jer. 15:21). The deliverance that Peter has in mind could be deliverance from idolatry or from the world – something they later returned to (2 Peter 2:22).

Although the doctrine of particular redemption is controversial and does present some difficulties, we should focus not so much on the difficulties as on the glorious fact that Christ came into this world with a specific mission – the salvation of those that God had chosen and given to him. He finished that work. It was 'mission accomplished'. Looking at it as believers, we can rejoice that Christ paid the penalty for our sins. He redeemed us; he purchased our salvation; he tasted death for us; he was our substitute and our Saviour. He guaranteed our eternal happiness.

Does that mean that Christ's death automatically brings us to heaven? No. There is another stage in God's plan to save sinners.

Homework

- 1. What does ‘atonement’ mean?
- 2. Define ‘redemption’. From what is the believer redeemed?
- 3. Define ‘propitiation’.
- 4. What does the Old Testament teach about sacrifice and the shedding of blood?
- 5. What did Jesus’ death accomplish in terms of God’s justice?
- 6. Answer the objection that the doctrine of particular redemption (that Christ died only for the elect) limits the value of the atonement?

4

An Effective Invitation – Invincible Grace

In stressing the trinitarian nature of salvation, we have so far seen the first two stages. The Father has planned salvation and chosen those who shall be saved: the Son has done everything necessary to purchase and secure that salvation for those whom the Father has chosen. That obviously leaves a gap, and it should raise a question; how does salvation get from the planning and purchasing stage to the stage where people actually benefit from salvation? Think in terms of a house. The architect draws up the plans; the builder buys the materials and erects the structure. But as yet no one lives there. The plans may be beautiful, the house itself is wonderfully constructed, but no one enjoys the benefits of living in it. This is said reverently but the plans of the Father and the atoning work of the Lord Jesus Christ do not actually bring anyone into God's kingdom. There remains one more vital activity – that of the Holy Spirit to bring people to a knowledge of God, or, in keeping with the approach we are taking – to bring sinners to an experience of salvation.

For someone to enjoy the benefits of salvation, a number of things must take place. The people who are to be saved must themselves come to the Lord; they must turn from their sins and believe in the Lord Jesus Christ. Salvation is by faith. However, as we saw in chapter 1, sinners are unable of themselves to turn to the Lord. They are deaf to the entreaties of the gospel; they cannot see the way of salvation because they are blind.

Indeed they are spiritually dead, so how can they come? The process of actually coming to Christ involves both a human and a divine side. This could not be said about election or the work of atonement for both those are solely God's work. Man plays no part whatever. But in coming to an experience of salvation, we are very much involved.

There are several expressions used to describe the process whereby we come to the Lord; conversion, repentance, faith, turning to God, coming to Christ, being born again. In the next chapter the human side of coming to the Lord will be examined, what we call conversion, but for now we will see the work of the Holy Spirit in bringing people to Christ.

One of the key words used for God's activity in this is 'calling'. Note the following passage: 'But you are a chosen people, a royal priesthood, a holy nation, a people belonging to God, that you may declare the praises of him who called you out of darkness into his wonderful light' (1 Peter 2:9). Peter says that God 'called' us out of darkness into his wonderful light. We have said that this is the work of the Holy Spirit. Here, as in most places where the term is used, the calling is attributed to God, but as we see what is involved in the process, it will be clear that it is specifically the work of the Holy Spirit.

What does this calling entail? It is a summons. It can be viewed as both an invitation and a command to come to Christ, and it is a calling that achieves its desired end – in this case, bringing the one called to actual faith in Christ. The Bible does speak of a general call that may not be responded to. Jesus said that '... Many are called (or invited), but few are chosen' (Matt. 22:14).

No one will need to be persuaded of the fact that many hear the gospel invitation but do not come to Christ. Perhaps an illustration will help. It is lunchtime. Little Carl is happily playing with his toys in the garden. Mother sends his teenage brother to call him in – 'Carl, come in now; lunch is ready.' Five minutes later there is no sign of Carl, he is still playing with his toys. Then his father goes out, says exactly the same words as his brother did, but Carl is inside in ten seconds! The first call was like a general call, not always responded to, but the second was an effective call – it achieved its desired end. In describing salvation, we often refer to the call that achieves its end as an 'effectual call'. The word 'called' is used about fifty times in this way in the New Testament.

Here is another example: 'And we know that in all things God works for the good of those who love him, who have been called according to his purpose. For those God foreknew he also predestined to be conformed to the likeness of his Son, that he might be the firstborn among many brothers. And those he predestined, he also called; those he called, he also justified; those he justified, he also glorified' (Rom. 8:28-30). The word 'called' is used three times here. There are three important things to note.

First: the calling is part of God's purpose. There is nothing haphazard here, for it involves the outworking of God's plan of salvation.

Second: calling is part of a chain or sequence; foreknowledge, predestination, calling, justification, glorification.

Third: the same group of people is involved at each stage. Described as 'those', the same group are the objects of all five of the stages from foreknowledge to predestination. There is no room for dropouts or for others to 'join the parade'. Those God foreknew, the same ones – 'those', no more and no less, he also predestined. Those God predestined, that is, chose or elected, the same ones, 'those', no more and no less, he also called, and so on. Calling then is the next stage in the sequence. Paul doesn't speak about the atonement here, but he might have said, 'Those God predestined he also redeemed, those he redeemed he also called.' The point is that God is dealing with the same group of people, the elect, at every stage. Therefore all who are chosen and redeemed will certainly be called, that is, brought to faith in Christ. We might also add that no one who is not elect will come to Christ.

What exactly is involved in calling? *The Westminster Shorter Catechism*, drawn up more than 350 years ago, has some excellent definitions of doctrine. We shall quote from it again in the course of our studies. In answer to the question 'What is effectual calling?' it sets out clearly the things that must happen before someone turns to Christ.

> Effectual calling is the work of God's Spirit, whereby, convincing us of our sin and misery, enlightening our minds in the knowledge of Christ, and renewing our wills, He does persuade and enable us to embrace Jesus Christ freely offered to us in the gospel (Question 31).

First: they must feel their sin. No one will ever seek a Saviour unless they realize their own sin. Jesus said he didn't come to call the righteous (Matt. 9:13), by which he meant those who considered themselves righteous, like the Pharisees. Because of our spiritual blindness we never face up to the reality of sin. We might acknowledge that we are not what we should be, but we will never see our sin as something offensive to God, until the Holy Spirit convicts us of our sin. That is one of his special functions. Speaking of the Holy Spirit as the Counsellor ('Comforter' KJV), Jesus said: 'When he comes, he will convict the world of guilt in regard to sin and righteousness and judgement' (John 16:8).

The degree of conviction will vary. Those addressed by Peter on the day of Pentecost were 'cut to the heart' (Acts 2:37). On the other hand we read of Lydia that 'the Lord opened her heart' (Acts 16:14). She seems to have been dealt with more gently by the Lord, so we cannot prescribe how much conviction a person must feel, nor how long they must endure it, but without that convicting work of the Spirit no one will see their need of a Saviour. Sadly in these days there is little preaching about sin, and people are often encouraged simply to 'come to Jesus' or to 'ask him into their hearts,' both of which can be done without any sense of sin.

Second: their minds must be enlightened. As we have seen, people are by nature blind to the things of God. The gospel is foolishness to them. They will never understand what it means to become a Christian unless the Holy Spirit enlightens them. Those 'without the Spirit' cannot understand the gospel (1 Cor. 2:14), but those with the Spirit can and do understand. When God is calling sinners to himself, the Holy Spirit opens their eyes and ears to the truth. This may happen quietly or dramatically, but someone will suddenly say, 'I see it now. Why didn't I understand this before?'

Third: their wills must be renewed. By nature we all say, '...We don't want this man to be our king' (Luke 19:14). We will not submit to God's commands. We will not obey the commands of the gospel to repent and believe. But when the Holy Spirit calls us there is a radical change. We see our sin, we see what Christ has done in providing salvation and we want to come to him – we do come to him.

The change that occurs and that brings about this willingness to turn to Christ is the new birth. Remember Jesus' words to Nicodemus: '...I tell you the truth, no one can see the kingdom of God unless he is born again' (John 3:3). '...You must be born again' (John 3:7). Nicodemus was a devout Jew; a very religious person; doubtless an upright man. He was eager to discuss religious matters with Jesus, but our Lord pointed out that before Nicodemus could even begin to understand anything of Jesus' miracles or teaching, he needed an inward change – he needed to be born again.

The same truth was given prophetically by Ezekiel about 600 years earlier: 'I will give you a new heart and put a new spirit in you; I will remove from you your heart of stone and give you a heart of flesh' (Ezek. 36:26)

In the new birth God imparts to us a new governing principle for our lives. It could crudely be likened to putting a new engine in a car. Most of us have at some time driven an old car that always struggled to get from point A to point B. Perhaps some have had the happy experience of putting a new engine in the vehicle. The transformation was dramatic. In the Bible this change is likened to a new creation (2 Cor. 5:17), so it is a very radical change.

The new birth is closely related to effectual calling. Calling would include the new birth but also the actual coming to Christ. One thing that is essential for effectual calling (and the new birth) is the gospel or the Word of God. 'For you have been born again, not of perishable seed, but of imperishable, through the living and enduring word of God' (1 Peter 1:23). '...For "Everyone who calls on the name of the Lord will be saved." How, then, can they call on the one they have not believed in? And how can they believe in the one of whom they have not heard? And how can they hear without someone preaching to them? And how can they preach unless they are sent? As it is written, "How beautiful are the feet of those who bring good news!" ...Consequently, faith comes from hearing the message, and the message is heard through the word of Christ' (Rom. 10:13-15, 17).

No one will ever be born again, or to look at it from the human side be converted, without the Word of God. The way in which the Word comes to a person may vary. It may be preached, spoken by an individual, heard over the radio or television, read in the Bible itself or a portion of it in a book or tract form. It may be through a verse memorized in Sunday school years before, but in some way or other the Word of God is always the instrument by which people are called.

That counters the accusations that the doctrines of God's

sovereign grace removes human responsibility, and if people are elect they will be converted whatever happens. God not only decides who will be saved, but plans all the means for their salvation, including hearing or reading the gospel. The last part of the catechism answer quoted earlier says that 'He does persuade and enable us to embrace Jesus Christ freely offered to us in the gospel.'

Another charge made against these truths, as noted earlier, is that they discourage evangelism. Not only is this not true, but evangelism is essential for gathering in those chosen and redeemed. When Paul preached the gospel in Antioch in Pisidia, he spoke first in the synagogue where some believed but there was also opposition. Thereafter he preached to the Gentiles. With what result? Many of them believed the gospel. And who were the ones that believed? Luke tells us: '...All who were appointed for eternal life believed' (Acts 13:48). This is an important verse. They were not appointed to eternal life (or elected) because they believed; they believed because they were appointed for eternal life. They were God's elect and the preaching of the gospel was the means of bringing them to an experimental knowledge of salvation.

How then are sinners actually brought to Christ? They hear the gospel or are exposed to it in some way. They are brought by the Holy Spirit to see their sin, to understand the truths of the gospel, and their hearts are changed so that they are made willing to repent and come to Christ. It is important to see that when people are brought to Christ they come willingly. They are not forced against their wills. They 'embrace Jesus Christ'. They gladly give themselves to him.

While this is what the Bible clearly teaches about the way in which sinners come to Christ, we have to acknowledge that many come to the Lord without understanding all this at the time. Charles Haddon Spurgeon, the great nineteenth century preacher, put it something like this:

> **I went through a door above which was written, 'Whosoever will may come', but after I went through and looked back, I saw written above the door, 'Chosen in Christ before the foundation of the world.'**

In other words, many may turn to the Lord thinking they come by their own free will, without realizing that they were drawn irresistibly by the Holy Spirit. God is gracious and does not insist that we fully understand all his ways before he will work in our lives. Doubtless there are some, who because of defective teaching, never understand in this life how much they owe to the Lord for their salvation. They will of course realize it in heaven.

One final question: what happens if a person who is one of the elect says 'no' to the invitation of the gospel? If we think back to what we saw in the first chapter *'What is man'*, we will remember that by nature we all say 'no'. 'There is... no one who seeks God' (Rom. 3:11). If God listened to our first response to the gospel, then none of us would ever be saved. Praise God, in the case of his elect, he doesn't take 'no' for an answer! As we saw, he makes us willing. Our minds and wills are changed so that we do come.

Some may find an illustration of a door to door salesman distasteful, but it can be helpful. Suppose a salesman comes to the door selling a vacuum cleaner. Your old one has just about worn out anyway, but your first response to the man is to put him off and get rid of him. You have a policy never to buy at the door. But as he talks he persuades you that this vacuum cleaner really is something special. He then persuades you to let him demonstrate it, and as he does so you see that it is indeed an amazing machine. It is quiet, efficient, well built and cleans the carpets, even picking up dog hairs far better than any vacuum cleaner you have ever seen. Furthermore, the price is right. So you buy it and never have a moment's regret. The product was marvellous, but your initial response was to reject it. However the man's persuasion brought you to realize the value of his machine. So it is with the gospel. The product is wonderful, but our natural reaction is always negative. However, as the Holy Spirit works in our hearts, he shows us our need of the gospel and persuades us to see the beauty and wonder of the Lord Jesus Christ and his saving grace.

Homework

- 1. What are some of the expressions used in the Bible to describe the great experience whereby a sinner comes to Christ?
- 2. Distinguish between a general call and an effectual call.
- 3. What three things must take place in a sinner's heart before he or she can come to Christ?
- 4. What is the first work of which sinners are usually conscious when the Lord is dealing with them?
- 5. What is the means invariably used in calling a sinner to Christ?
- 6. What is the agent (effective force) used in calling a sinner to Christ?
- 7. What is the 'new heart' promised in Ezekiel 36:26?
- 8. In your own words define effectual calling in one sentence.
- 9. What happens when a sinner says 'No' to God's call?

5

Turning Around – Conversion

In the last chapter we looked at the Shorter Catechism's definition of effectual calling. The last phrase of Question 31 says: …'He [God] does persuade and enable us to embrace Jesus Christ freely offered to us in the gospel.' We stressed God's sovereignty in bringing us to himself – God convinces us of our sin; he enlightens our minds; he renews our wills. But the fact remains that '*we* embrace Jesus Christ', that is we come to him; we turn to him; we believe in him. Whatever view we take of God's activity in drawing us to himself, we are certainly not passive – we do not just sit back and do nothing.

We also considered the new birth in the last chapter. A baby has no control over its birth. It is conceived, it grows in the womb and then is born with no exercise of its own will. However the child will not go through life as a puppet. It has life. It has a will that develops and it gives every indication of life even before its birth. So it is with the Christian. Regeneration or the new birth illustrates a vital area of salvation, and it is totally God's work. But it is only one side of the coin, and, be assured, there are two sides – a human side as well as a divine side. Taking the analogy of birth one-step further, when a baby is born there are signs of life. It soon cries, it moves, it feeds. When God has brought a person to newness of life, he gives them a new heart, but there are immediately signs of life; there are things that indicate that something wonderful has happened to them. In very general terms there is a change in the life – a turning around. This is often referred to as conversion. Those who turn to the Lord are said to be converted. Every Christian has been converted; he or she has turned to the Lord. Conversion can be divided into two parts – repentance and faith. Both of these involve turning, although one is negative – turning from sin, and the other is positive – turning to Christ.

When Paul was before King Agrippa, giving an account of himself and his ministry, he said: '…I was not disobedient to the vision from heaven. First to those in Damascus, then to those in Jerusalem and in all Judea, and to the Gentiles also, I preached that men should repent and turn to God and prove their repentance by their deeds' (Acts 26:19,20).

Although the actual words that Paul preached might have varied each time, there was a consistent pattern in his message. He told both Jews and Gentiles that they needed to repent and also to turn to God. These are the two sides of conversion. We see the two things together again in Acts 20:2. Paul is telling the elders of the church in Ephesus about his ministry there: 'I have declared to both Jews and Greeks that they must turn to God in repentance and have faith in our Lord Jesus.' Let us look at these two parts of conversion.

Repentance

The New Oxford Dictionary of English describes 'repentance' as: 'to feel or express true regret or remorse about one's wrongdoing or sin'. How do unconverted people think about sin? If they think about it at all they may accept that is something not very good, but after all, everyone sins don't they? Normally we don't think of sin as very bad, unless it means some dreadful crime. People also think of sin in terms of its social effects. If someone is killed or robbed, people are badly hurt and the offenders should be brought to justice. But who ever thinks of sin in relation to God? When a person truly repents, he or she sees their sin as an offence against God. The prodigal son is a good illustration of this. We read of him: 'When he came to his senses, he said, "How many of my father's hired servants have food to spare, and here I am starving to death! I will set out and go back to my father and say to him: Father, I have sinned against heaven and against you"'(Luke 15:17,18).

True repentance then is more than an expression of regret or even remorse: it must also involve a change of feeling. This is seen in the parable of the prodigal son. He felt himself unworthy to be called his father's son (verse 19). The depth of feeling about sin will vary from person to person. This is the Holy Spirit's work as we saw in the previous chapter. Sometimes people may be under deep conviction of sin for months or even years, while some seem only to have a general sense of sin and that for only a brief time. We are justified in looking for some sorrow for sin, but we mustn't make the mistake of expecting everyone to have exactly the same experience. In some circles prospective church members are supposed to give an account of deep conviction of sin that lasted for some lengthy period of time, but the Lord does not deal with everyone in the same way.

Repentance also involves the will. Once again the prodigal shows this. He said: 'I will set out and go back to my father…' (verse 18). There was more than sorrow for his sin, there was the determination to actually do something about it. A lot of people are sorry for their sins, at least for the trouble their sins get them into, but they never come to the place of decision to abandon their sins. When the Lord was bringing the plagues on Egypt, Pharaoh on more than one occasion said 'I have sinned', (Exod. 9:27, 10:16), but his remorse never produced any change in his actions. So we need to add one more stage – repentance involves the actions. In Acts 26:19,20, Paul insisted in his preaching not only that men repent, but that they: 'Prove their repentance by their deeds.' Many a person has fully intended to abandon their sins, but without any change of behaviour. Nothing less than an actual turning from sin constitutes repentance. Once more the parable of the prodigal son shows this – he actually went home to his father.

Someone who has repented will have seen the awfulness of their sin. They will have realized that they have sinned against God as well as against man. They will have understood that their sins, if not forgiven, will sink them into hell. The Holy Spirit will not only have convicted them of their sin but also caused them to confess it to God in order to know the forgiveness he promises. They will have felt keenly that God was grieved over their sinning against him, and they will have turned wholeheartedly from their sin.

Repentance is not optional

Repentance is not something that we have the luxury of rejecting. In one sense it is true that people may refuse to repent, but the results of that are too terrible to contemplate. It was not just men like the apostles who commanded people to repent; it is God Himself who gives that command: '...He [God] commands all men everywhere to repent' (Acts 17:30). It is interesting to note the first words recorded of Jesus in His public preaching: 'From that time on Jesus began to preach, 'Repent, for the kingdom of heaven is near' (Matt. 4:17).

When John the Baptist had earlier begun his ministry, he proclaimed exactly the same words (Matt. 3:2), and when Jesus sent his disciples out to preach, it was with the same message (Mark 6:12). It is not surprising then that after Pentecost, when the Holy Spirit had filled the apostles and they preached with great power, the note of repentance was regularly found in their preaching. Peter preached on the day of Pentecost, and after many of his listeners were convicted of their sin and cried out in anguish asking what they should do, Peter replied: '... Repent and be baptized every one of you...' (Acts 2:38).

It is clear then that repentance is important for two reasons. It is an essential part of the gospel message; and it is also one of the indications of a genuine work of God in the heart. We may not reduce the gospel message to 'believe in Jesus'; nor may we assume that because someone says that they believe in Jesus that they are necessarily converted. It does seem evident that the note of repentance is not heard much these days in gospel preaching.

We mentioned earlier that the gospel is often reduced to an invitation to 'ask Jesus into your heart.' Those who would defend this approach usually defend it by appealing to Revelation 3:20: 'Here I am! I stand at the door and knock. If anyone hears my voice and opens the door, I will come in and eat with him, and he with me.' A lot has been written on this passage. Some point out that the invitation was to a church, and therefore it is inappropriate to apply it to unbelievers. Others respond that although the words were addressed to a church, there was little evidence of life and therefore they were being treated as unbelievers. Certainly the Puritans used the passage to challenge unbelievers. However they did not assume that it was within the natural ability of unbelievers to open their hearts to Christ, and the passage was preached in connection with a command to repent. Certainly if an invitation is given to 'receive Christ', it must never be done apart from repentance.

The evidence of repentance

How do we know that someone has repented? We cannot be certain; we must remember that we are not infallible; only God sees the heart. But as we saw earlier, Paul did preach that people should '...Prove their repentance by their deeds' (Acts 26:20).

If someone has repented we should expect to see a change. We should see them turning from sin. But we cannot turn from sin without a subsequent step. Turning from sin is always accompanied by a turning to the Lord. Repentance is always accompanied by faith, and it is to the second part of conversion that we now turn.

Faith

Repentance and faith can be likened to Siamese twins – I am thinking of the days when they could not be separated surgically. Each had its own identity, but you never saw one without the other. They were inseparable. Repentance and faith are like that. They are not the same. They can be defined in quite different terms, as we have done. One is a turning from sin; the other is a turning to Christ; but one is never found without the other. People will never truly believe unless they have seen their sins; neither will they turn from their sins unless they have seen Christ and the true meaning of the cross.

What then is faith? Obviously it is believing, but just as repentance is not just changing one's mind about anything, so faith, as far as the gospel is concerned, is not just believing anything but believing in Christ.

The object of faith

One of the best known verses in the Bible is John 3:16: 'For God so loved the world that he gave his one and only Son, that whoever believes in him shall not perish but have eternal life.' The way to salvation, to eternal life, to avoid perishing, is by believing in God's Son. This is so important to grasp. We do not become Christians by being good. We do not become children of God by being born into a Christian family. We are saved by faith in Jesus Christ. He is always the focus of the true believer. After all we are 'Christians', and Christ is central in the gospel. *The Shorter Catechism* puts it well. In answer to the question, 'What is faith in Jesus Christ?' we are told:

> Faith in Jesus Christ is a saving grace, whereby we receive and rest upon him alone for salvation, as he is set forth in the gospel (Question 69).

The answer speaks about receiving Christ and resting upon him. There are several ways in which faith in Christ is expressed in the New Testament and it would be helpful now to look at some of them.

Receiving Christ: John speaks of this near the beginning of his gospel. Referring to Christ he writes: 'Yet to all who received him, to those who believed in his name, he gave the right to become children of God' (John 1:12). When we receive something we simply accept it from the giver. Whether it is the cheque for our salary or a birthday present, we just take it – gratefully. In the gospel, salvation in Jesus Christ is offered to us. There is nothing to pay, we simply receive him and the forgiveness he has obtained for us through his death.

Resting on Christ: Here is the idea of confidence or trust. A person who is old or frail will use a walking stick or they might lean on the arm of someone when they walk. They cannot trust their own strength. When we rest on Christ we rely on him rather than our own merits or abilities. We trust him to save us and keep us; we have confidence in him. (see Rom. 9:33)

Coming to Christ: Jesus himself invited people to come to him: 'Come to me all you who are weary and burdened, and I will give you rest' (Matt. 11:28). Elsewhere he said: '...I am the bread of life, he who comes to me will never go hungry, and he who believes in me will never be thirsty' (John 6:35). The latter verse shows that believing in Jesus and coming to him amount to the same thing. Coming involves a move from one place to another. If a mother says to her little daughter, 'Come here', the girl is required to move from wherever she is to her mother. When we respond to Jesus' invitation to come to him, we move from our present situation of sin and rebellion to go to him, not literally of course, but by faith we go to him to receive the benefits of salvation. In the first of the verses quoted above the person coming to Jesus finds rest for the soul; in the second they find that which satisfies their spiritual hunger and thirst – their longing to know Christ and be right with God.

Looking to Christ: Charles Haddon Spurgeon, referred to earlier, was converted through hearing a sermon by an uneducated man on the verse that in the King James Version reads: 'Look unto me and be saved, all the ends of the earth…' (Isa. 45:22). The New International Version has: 'turn to me…' but the sense of the old version is correct. We sometimes speak of looking to a person for help when we are unable to do something or understand something ourselves. When we have seen our sin and God's wrath against it, we need to look to Christ to rescue us from that wrath. He never disappoints us.

Other expressions sometimes used as equivalents to faith are: yielding to Christ, surrendering to Christ, laying hold of Christ. They all convey the idea that we see in Jesus Christ the answer to every need and recognize that we must submit to him and follow him. Christ is the object of our faith.

The nature of faith

But what about the nature of our faith? We believe that planet earth is a sphere. Most of us have not been in space to see this for ourselves, but we have seen pictures and believe what scientists and astronauts have told us. The evidence is overwhelming so we accept it intellectually. Is faith in Christ like that? Some would claim that it is. Most certainly faith involves the mind. A person cannot believe without knowledge. But what must we know about Christ in order to believe in the biblical sense? Actually we need to go back a little. Why do we believe in Christ? – because we have seen our sin and realized that we are under God's wrath and condemnation. But why is God angry with us? – because we have broken his laws. There is a logical sequence of facts here. We will not turn to Christ without seeing our sin; and we will never see our sin unless we have understood who God is and what he requires of us.

In his excellent book, *Evangelism and the Sovereignty of God*, J. I. Packer defines the gospel in four stages:

- **1.** a message about God;
- **2.** a message about sin;
- **3.** a message about Christ;
- **4.** a call to repent and believe.

To be a Christian one must believe in God, that is that he exists and is the mighty creator of heaven and earth. As the writer to the Hebrews puts it: '...Anyone who comes to him must believe that he exists and that he rewards those who earnestly seek him' (Heb. 11:6).

We cannot insist that a new believer have a full understanding of all God's attributes, but at least there must be some awareness of what God is like and what he requires of us. Faith needs to begin with God. When people know something of the character of God – his power, wisdom, holiness and goodness, then they can move on to a consideration of Christ and the gospel.

Most certainly people must believe in Jesus Christ to be converted. Here again it is hard to be specific about all the details that must be believed. People vary in their mental abilities and in their backgrounds, so not everyone will believe exactly the same things. But we must believe that Jesus is the Son of God and that will include His deity and true humanity. It seems reasonable to insist that faith means accepting all that the Bible teaches about Jesus even if there is not a full understanding. His virgin birth, sinless life, miracles, teaching, death and resurrection all form a vital part of the gospel. However although these events are essential elements that we must believe, faith must also understand the meaning of these events. In particular the significance of Jesus' death must be believed. Not every detail of the atonement must be grasped but there must be at least some understanding of the connection between the cross and forgiveness. Faith brings forgiveness: '...Everyone who believes in him receives forgiveness of sins through his name' (Acts 10:43).

The true believer will see that they are forgiven and saved because of Jesus and His death on the cross. Faith definitely involves the mind. But faith, like repentance is not just intellectual. It involves the whole person. To speak of faith involving the emotions is perhaps dangerous. Emotions are changeable and not always reliable. What we feel about Christ will vary from hour to hour. However we must believe in the heart: 'For it is with your heart that you believe and are justified...' (Rom. 10:10).

Perhaps the key word here is 'trust', a concept we touched on earlier. The believer trusts in Christ. There is a confidence in him and his ability to save and keep. There is always a danger that faith will go no further than the mind. An often repeated illustration might be helpful. Several decades ago a man named Blondin was well known for his stunts. Once he had a cable put in place across Niagara Falls. He would walk across the cable, performing various feats for the entertainment of the spectators. He would also push a wheelbarrow across the cable with some brave person sitting in it. He is reputed once to have asked a man watching his act, 'Do you believe that I can walk across that cable?' 'Certainly', said the man. 'Do you believe I can push a wheelbarrow across it?' 'Yes', he replied. 'Do you believe I could push the wheelbarrow across with someone sitting in it?' 'Yes, I've seen you do it.' 'Do you believe I could push the barrow across with you in it?' 'I'm sure you could,' he responded. 'Alright, jump in!' 'No thank you!' was the hasty reply. In that story (true or fictitious), we see very easily the difference between intellectual faith and trust. The man believed that Blondin could do all those things including pushing him across Niagara Falls in a wheelbarrow, but he wasn't willing to entrust himself to Blondin.

Many have a faith just like that. They believe that Jesus died on the cross to save sinners, but they are unwilling to jump in the wheelbarrow, that is, they are unwilling to commit their lives to Christ and trust Him for their salvation. Their faith is in their head, but they never have a true experience of Christ and salvation. I once saw a tract entitled *'Missing Heaven by Eighteen Inches.'* The title certainly got my attention. How is it possible to miss heaven by such a small distance? The eighteen inches referred to was the distance between the head and the heart. The message of the tract was to point out that 'head faith' alone will not get a person to heaven. The heart must be involved as well as we have already seen in Romans 10:9,10. 'Heart faith' surely involves trust as well as intellectual faith.

Faith also involves the will. Here again we need to be cautious because our works do not in any way secure our salvation, but Paul speaks of: '...The obedience that comes from faith' (Romans 1:5). We are not saved by our obedience – we will see more of that in the next chapter, but faith involves obedience in the sense that there is a commitment of our lives to serve and obey Christ. Faith involves the whole person.

Just in case anyone thinks I am making faith too complicated, consider these words from John: 'Now while he was in Jerusalem at the Passover Feast, many saw the miraculous signs he was doing and believed in his name. But Jesus would not entrust himself to them, for he knew all men' (John 2:23,24). The word used here for believing is the same as used elsewhere for genuine faith, but it is clear here that Jesus did not consider the faith of these people to be genuine. We find a similar situation in John 8:30,31 where those who 'believed' later sought to stone Jesus. They 'believed' but their faith did not satisfy Jesus. There is a genuine faith and there is a faith that is counterfeit, so we need to be sure that our faith is not just intellectual, nor merely emotional. It needs all the elements we have mentioned.

This matter can be approached from another direction. In whom do we believe? In Christ. I have heard faith defined as the commitment of the whole man to a whole Christ. Christ is the Greek word meaning the 'Anointed One'; the same as the Hebrew word 'Messiah'. Anointing was a process of pouring oil upon a person as an indication of their inauguration into an office. British monarchs are anointed to this day. In the Old Testament there were three offices into which people were installed by anointing – prophet, priest and king. It is helpful to think of Christ in this three-fold office of prophet, priest and king. As prophet he brings God's Word to us. As priest he offered himself as a sacrifice for sins and now intercedes for us. As king he rules over us in God's kingdom.

Now whether we think of faith as believing in Christ or receiving Christ, we believe in him in his whole person and in all his offices. We receive a whole Christ, not parts of him. We cannot receive him just as a prophet to bring the gospel to us and as a priest who has sacrificed himself for us; we must also receive him as king to rule over us. To refuse to submit to Christ's authority is like saying to Christ, 'Thank you for dying for me. I would like to have my sins forgiven. Please come into my life, but would you mind removing your crown before you come in?' That would be an affront to the Lord. We must receive him in all his offices or not at all. So both repentance and faith involve our whole being. Christ gave himself wholly for us, and we must give ourselves wholly to him.

One other thing should be noted. We said earlier in this chapter that repenting and believing are things that we must do, God does not repent or believe for us. That is true, but it is also true that we cannot do them by ourselves. Both repentance and faith are gifts of God. Note the following: '…So then, God has granted even the Gentiles repentance unto life' (Acts 11:18). 'For it is by grace you have been saved, through faith – and this not from yourselves, it is the gift of God –' (Eph. 2:8).

Repentance is essential for salvation. The Gentiles had to repent before they could be saved, but they could not repent unless God granted them this grace. Likewise with faith. We cannot be saved without faith, we must believe, yet we cannot believe unless God grants the gift of faith. As we saw in the catechism question quoted earlier, faith is a saving grace, so is repentance.

Balance is important at this point. When we urge people to repent and believe in Jesus Christ, we may be conscious of the fact that they cannot do it without the enabling grace of God, but we must not allow this to detract from the fact that God graciously invites all people to repent and believe. In presenting the gospel we must plead with people to come to Christ, assuring them of acceptance when they come.

Come ye sinners, poor and needy,
Weak and wounded, sick and sore;
Jesus ready stands to save you,
Full of pity, love and power:
He is able,
He is willing; doubt no more.

Now ye needy, come and welcome;
God's free bounty glorify:
True belief and true repentance,
Every grace that brings you nigh,

Without money,
Come to Jesus Christ and buy.

Let not conscience make you linger,
Nor of fitness fondly dream;
All the fitness He requireth
Is to feel your need of Him:
This He gives you –
'Tis the Spirit's rising beam.

Come, ye weary, heavy-laden,
Lost and ruined by the Fall;
If you wait until you're better,
You will never come at all:
Not the righteous –
Sinners, Jesus came to call.
Joseph Hart (1712-68)

Homework

- 1. What is the relationship between regeneration and conversion?
- 2. Define repentance?
- 3. Are tears a sign of true repentance? Why not?
- 4. What is the evidence of true repentance?
- 5. What are some of the ways in which faith in Christ is described in the New Testament?
- 6. How much must a person believe about Christ for their faith to be genuine?
- 7. What is the source of repentance? Of faith? Give Scripture references.

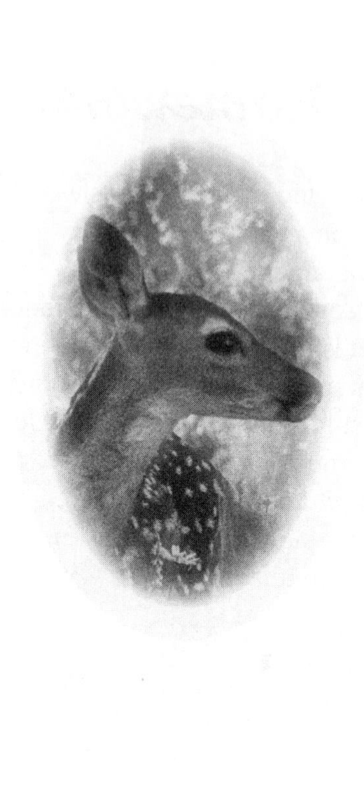

6

Not Guilty – Justification

Let us see where we have come to in tracing God's plan to save sinners. Following the sequence of Chapters 1 to 5, we have seen that mankind is universally sinful. Their sin bars them from God's presence and puts them under his condemnation; but God the Father in mercy chose certain people to be saved. The Son of God, Jesus Christ, came into this world and died on the cross to provide atonement for the sins of those chosen by the Father. The Holy Spirit works in the hearts of those chosen and redeemed; renews them spiritually and brings them to repentance and faith. Let us change from the third person to the first – as true believers in the Lord Jesus Christ, where do we stand at that point? Simply put, we are right with God. Before we were wrong in every way, now we are right with him. The key word here is justification. We are justified before God. We mentioned this briefly in Chapter 3; now it is time to enlarge on this truth.

Job in the midst of his afflictions and arguments with his friends, asked an important question: '…How can a mortal be righteous before God?' (Job 9:2). That is a far-reaching question. How can those who are sinners by birth, nature and practice, be righteous in God's sight? Let us seek to answer that question even though it will mean retracing some of our steps.

The meaning of justification

To be justified is to be declared righteous: to be accounted upright. Although today it has various other meanings, justification is primarily a legal term and needs to be approached from a legal standpoint. Suppose a crime has been committed. Someone is charged with the offence. After all the evidence has been considered the person is either found guilty and condemned, or declared not guilty and justified. If the latter, the charge against the person is dropped. Everything revolves around the law. A law has been enacted by the governing body of the nation and if it is broken justice must be upheld. If someone is charged with the offence, he or she must be tried in a court of law. If guilty, then the appropriate punishment must be meted out. If not guilty the person will be acquitted. If someone is justified, the law has no claim on the accused. No guilt is ascribed and no punishment is due.

As this is applied to the sinner, the laws which have been broken are God's laws. Those charged with these offences are sinners – all of us. It is not hard to see how we would be found guilty and punished by a just God, but the amazing fact is that those who believe in Jesus Christ are justified before God. They are not guilty: they are seen righteous by God.

The need of justification

Job's question is a compelling one. How can we be righteous in God's sight? God has given us his laws and we have broken them. We have already established the fact that without exception we are sinners and therefore guilty before God. As God in justice must punish sin, if we are left to ourselves we are in a hopeless condition. We cannot plead 'not guilty' because that would not be true, and even if we claimed innocence, God knows we are guilty. Our plight is terrible: absolutely without hope. Unless we can somehow be found righteous, we are condemned to an eternity in hell. Our need of justification is very great.

The nature of justification

The believer is justified, that is, he or she is declared righteous by God. What does this mean? Note Paul's words as he preached in Antioch: 'Therefore my brothers, I want you to know that through Jesus the forgiveness of sins is proclaimed to you. Through him everyone who believes is justified from everything you could not be justified from by the law of Moses' (Acts 13:38,39).

In these verses justification is linked with forgiveness. As guilty sinners in God's sight we need forgiveness. Our sins must be removed from the divine record. By faith they are. God forgives us all our sins. To a sinful woman who wept in repentance Jesus said: '...Your sins are forgiven' (Luke 7:48). Her sins were great but Jesus' forgiveness matched her sins. There are many expressions to convey the scale of forgiveness. Our sins are said to be removed as far as the east is from the west (Ps. 103:12). They are hurled into the depths of the sea (Micah 7:19). They are put behind God's back (Isa. 38:17). They are swept away like a morning mist (Isa. 44:22). They are remembered no more (Jer. 31:34). Some of these are figures of speech but they show how thorough our forgiveness is. The word often used in the Old Testament for forgiveness means 'picked up and carried away'. John Bunyan in Pilgrim's Progress gives a good picture of the removal of sins. The main character, Christian, has been carrying a great bundle or burden on his back – a picture of his sin. He tries several ways to get rid of it and even follows bad advice from some, but all to no avail. Finally he comes to the cross where the bundle falls off by itself, rolls down a hill and into a tomb. What a relief he feels! How he weeps for joy! When our sins are forgiven what relief we should feel; what joy we should experience because all our sins, past, present and future are removed – they are gone forever.

There are some who teach that when we come to Christ, only past sins, that is, sins we have committed to that point, are forgiven. Then each time we sin after conversion we must come to God in confession to get our forgiveness updated. It is certainly true that we should come to the Lord and confess each time we sin. This is important to maintain fellowship with the Lord and to keep our consciences clear, but our confession is not to get justified over again. For one thing there are times when we do not even realize that we have sinned. If our salvation depended on knowing each sin and confessing it, no one would be saved. When Christ died, we were not born, and so had not committed any personal sins. He died for all our sins and therefore that would include the sins we have not yet committed. That should never make us casual about sin because all of our sins contributed to Christ's sufferings. We need to keep a tender conscience and always confess our sins where we are aware of them, but that should not detract from the glorious truth that all our sins are totally forgiven and are remembered no more. Not that God is forgetful – he knows everything, but he does not hold our sins against us. He deliberately refuses to consider our sins once we are forgiven.

Wonderful as forgiveness is, it is only part of justification. An illustration may be helpful here. Suppose I shop regularly at a particular grocery store. For weeks on end I cannot pay, but the owner is patient and allows me to accumulate a debt for the groceries I take home. My debt increases until finally he says to me, 'I'm sorry but you cannot shop here any more until you pay your debt.' I am in a mess. What can I do? While thinking of my predicament a friend comes along and asks the store owner, 'How much does Mr. Fellows owe?' '£2000' he replies. Much to my delight my friend writes a cheque for the full amount. How generous! I am walking on air until next week when I come to get more groceries. Once more I have no money. What will the shopkeeper say? You see the problem.

Now suppose at the point of being denied my groceries because of my debt, my friend comes along and says to the owner of the store, 'Here is a cheque for Mr. Fellows' account.' In amazement the owner sees that the cheque is for one billion pounds. Not only will that pay my debt but it will ensure that never again can I go into debt. Justification is like that. It provides forgiveness but even more, it gives us a perfect righteousness so that never again can anything be laid to our charge as far as God is concerned. That is why Paul, after explaining the great truth of justification can say so confidently: 'Who will bring any charge against those whom God has chosen? It is God who justifies. Who is he that condemns?...' (Rom. 8:33,34).

God not only looks upon us as those who are forgiven, but also as those who can never go into debt as far as his law is concerned. Sin is sometimes viewed as a debt. Matthew's version of the Lord's Prayer has 'forgive us our debts' (Matt. 6:12). Perhaps a way to understand this better is to take as an example the sixth commandment – 'You shall not murder.' What does that demand of us? An obvious answer is that we refrain from taking someone's life, but Jesus also showed that it covered murder in the heart, that is, hatred (Matt. 5:21,22). It actually goes one step farther than hatred because the law also said: '...but love your neighbour as yourself...' (Lev. 19:18). Not only does the law prohibit us from murdering or hating others, but it also requires us to love them in order to keep the commandment perfectly. If we do not kill, but fail to love, we are still in debt. The same principle can be applied to virtually all the commandments. We have committed adultery or at least lusted, and not loved our spouses as we ought. We have stolen and we have failed to meet the needs of others. We have lied and we have failed to speak the truth.

So how does this relate to the subject of this chapter? Justification addresses our lawbreaking by granting forgiveness, but it also addresses our need to fulfil the commandments by declaring us righteous. God not only looks on us as if we had not sinned, he also sees us as if we had perfectly kept all his commandments all our life. That is an amazing thought isn't it?

The permanence of justification

This will be expanded in a later chapter, but it is appropriate to mention here. When God declares a sinner righteous, it is for ever. Based, as we have seen on Christ's work on the cross, it is not related to our behaviour before conversion. It is '...apart from observing the law' (Rom. 3:28). Neither is it based upon our behaviour after conversion. Caution is needed at this point, and we will also see in a later chapter that those who are justified are also sanctified, that is, made holy; but nevertheless our justification and final salvation have nothing to do with our deeds. If, as we have seen, no charge can be laid against those whom God has chosen (Rom. 8:33), then it must be impossible for us to lose our justified state. If it were based on our works, then we might indeed lose our salvation, but as it is based upon Christ's work and God's declaration that we are justified, then we are secure in Christ

The ground of justification

What is the source of this perfect righteousness that is imputed to us? It is Jesus Christ. We have already seen that his death on the cross atones for our sins and provides forgiveness for us, but there is another aspect of Christ's work that is not so often spoken or written about. It is his righteousness that is imputed to us. Note the following passages: 'God made him who had no sin to be sin for us, so that in him we might become the righteousness of God' (2 Cor. 5:21). 'For just as through the disobedience of the one man the many were made sinners, so also through the obedience of the one man the many will be made righteous' (Rom. 5:19).

In the first passage Paul is speaking of a great exchange: our sin for divine righteousness. Our sin was imputed to Christ when he died, and his righteousness was imputed to us when we believed.

In the second, the apostle is comparing the effects of Adam's disobedience and Christ's obedience. Both were far-reaching. Paul views all people as belonging to one of two races: Adam's or Christ's. Everyone belongs to Adam's race by nature and people only change races and become Christ's by conversion. The effect of Adam's disobedience was to make all his race sinners, and the effect of Christ's obedience was to make all his race righteous. A better translation would be 'constituted righteous' instead of 'made righteous'. We are not made righteous in justification, just as Christ was not made sinful on the cross. He was seen and treated as if he were sinful. So we are accounted or imputed righteous. We are regarded as righteous and treated as if we were righteous by God. Christ's obedience would include everything he ever did in this world from the cradle to the cross. It would certainly include keeping all God's commandments, and this was reckoned to us. The apostolic writers insisted that Christ was sinless, and Jesus himself claimed perfect obedience to God's commandments. Here are two examples: '...I have obeyed my Father's commands and remain in his love' (John 15:10). 'For we do not have a high priest who is unable to sympathize with our weaknesses, but we have one who has been tempted in every way, just as we are – yet was without sin' (Heb. 4:15). In the first verse, Jesus is speaking, and in the second, the writer to the Hebrews is speaking about Jesus. He was sinless. He kept all God's commands perfectly. There are several reasons why Jesus had to be sinless.

First: he had to be sinless to show that he was God. How could anyone less than perfect claim to be divine? He would have no credibility at all if he sinned.

Second: he had to be sinless in order to qualify as our sin bearer. If he had sins of his own he would have to be punished for those and would be unable to die for our sins. In the Old Testament sacrificial system which always looked ahead to Jesus as the one final sacrifice for sins, the animals had to be without defect typifying the perfection of Jesus (Exod. 12:5, Lev. 1:3).

Third: Jesus had to be perfect so that his righteousness could be imputed to us. We broke God's commandments, but he kept them on our behalf.

The two aspects of Christ's work, his death on the cross and his perfect obedience to God's commandments, are often referred to by theologians as the passive and active obedience of Christ. His passive obedience was exhibited on the cross. He hung there and endured the wrath of God. His active obedience was exhibited throughout his earthly life as he kept the commandments on a daily basis. Because of Christ's passive obedience we are forgiven, and because of his active obedience we are declared righteous.

Returning to the thought of how God sees the Christian; he sees us as if we had never sinned and also as if we had always kept his commandments. In fact he sees us as righteous as the Lord Jesus Christ himself. That is a staggering fact. God does not see us somewhat better than we were before – he sees us perfectly righteous in Christ. Hallelujah!

The means of justification

The Bible is clear on this point; it is by faith. 'This righteousness from God comes through faith in Jesus Christ to all who believe...' (Rom. 3:22). 'For we maintain that a man is justified by faith apart from observing the law' (Rom. 3:28). 'We... know that a man is not justified by observing the law, but by faith in Jesus Christ...' (Gal. 2:15,16).

In his letter to the Romans, Paul also declares that justification by faith is not only a New Testament phenomenon. He gives the examples of Abraham and David and shows that both were justified by faith (See Rom. 4:1-3, 6-8). Frequently in Romans Paul is at pains to stress that justification is by faith as opposed to law. Many in the Jewish community sought to establish their own righteousness before God (Rom. 10:3). Paul demonstrates the impossibility of this by showing that all have sinned – Jews and Gentiles (Rom. 3:9-12, 23) and concludes: 'Therefore no one will be declared righteous in his sight by observing the law...' (Rom. 3:20).

It is by faith alone that we are saved; that we are justified. The great battle of the Protestant Reformation was fought primarily over the issue of how a person is justified before God. The Church of Rome said it was by works and ritual, although they never denied the importance of faith. The Reformers like Luther, Zwingle, Calvin, Knox, Latimer and others insisted that justification was by faith and faith alone. As we noted above: 'For we maintain that a man is justified by faith apart from observing the law' (Rom. 3:28).

The fruit of justification

Justification is not merely a doctrine to store in our minds for understanding; it is a truth that should affect the way we live. This is true of every doctrine of the Christian faith, and this doctrine in particular should have a profound effect on us.

It should fill us with gratitude: God Almighty has had mercy upon us. We deserve eternal punishment, yet he has forgiven us and made us righteous in his sight. Not a day should pass without an expression of our gratitude to him who has cleansed us from sin and reconciled us to himself.

It should give us peace: Paul wrote: 'Therefore, since we have been justified through faith, we have peace with God through our Lord Jesus Christ' (Rom. 5:1). Peace of mind is widely sought and seldom found. I have rarely heard an unbeliever claim to have peace of mind. It may be argued that the peace spoken of by Paul in the verse just quoted is not a subjective peace of mind, but a state of peace with God. That is true but the two are closely linked, and a state of peace will produce peace of mind. Some of you have lived through a war and know the fear and anxiety that such times can produce, but also the inward peace and relief when a state of peace is declared. What greater turmoil than guilt and the fear of being at enmity with God? What greater peace than knowing his wrath is turned aside and our sins are forgiven?

It should give us joy: Paul said in the same passage just quoted: '...We rejoice in hope of the glory of God' (Rom. 5:2). It is a joy that is known even in our sufferings (verse 3), because nothing can take away our blessings in Christ or separate us from God's love. To know that we are right with God and one day will be with him in glory is surely cause for great joy.

It should give us assurance: This is closely related to peace. Listen to the words of the apostle John: 'I write these things to you who believe in the name of the Son of God so that you may know that you have eternal life' (1 John 5:13).

The key word here is ***'know'***. Many ***'hope'*** they are saved;

they would like to think they are going to heaven when they die. John says we can know that we have eternal life. There are some who say we can never be sure of salvation: they say it is presumptuous to claim assurance, but the Scriptures deny that. We can and should have assurance. Paul said: 'For I am convinced that neither death nor life, neither angels nor demons, neither the present nor the future, nor any powers, neither height nor depth, nor anything else in all creation, will be able to separate us from the love of God that is in Christ Jesus our Lord' (Rom. 8:38,39). Paul sounds very confident doesn't he?

Assurance comes basically from taking God at his word. He says that if we believe we are saved (Acts 16:31); we accept that. He says that if we confess our sins, he will forgive us (1 John 1:9); we believe that. Actually assurance has three strands:

First: The promises of the gospel, such as those quoted above.

Second: Holinessof life: In the verse quoted earlier, 1 John 5:13, 'these things' that John wrote about were a series of tests by which his readers could assess themselves: things like keeping God's commandments (chapter 2:4); walking as Jesus did (chapter 2:6); loving their brothers (chapter 2:9, 3:14). No one is entitled to assurance who is not living to please the Lord.

Third: The witness of the Spirit: 'The Spirit himself testifies with our spirit that we are God's children' (Rom. 8:16). This is not easy to define. As the Scots say, 'Better felt than telt'. It is subjective, but believers experience an inner conviction that they are God's children through this mysterious witness of the Holy Spirit.

These strands are like the legs of a three-legged stool: all three are necessary for balance. We will not have a God-given assurance if we claim the promises but do not walk in holiness. If we earnestly seek to please God but do not believe his promises, we will not have assurance either, and we will not know the Spirit's witness unless we have the other two strands. Putting the three together it is wonderful to know that we are justified and that '...There is now no condemnation for those who are in Christ Jesus (Rom. 8:1).

The doctrine of justification should make us holy. The whole area of holiness or sanctification will be dealt with more fully in chapter 8, but for now it is good to make the point that knowing we are right with God should make us want to please him. One of the hardest things about living a life obedient to the Lord is motivation. The reason the law of Moses could never save anyone is that under the law we lack both the power and the motivation to obey God. Unless we are converted we do not have the Holy Spirit's power to help us, and we do not have the right motivation. Those trying to be saved by the keeping the commandments are motivated only by fear – unless they are obedient they will be lost. As believers the question of our salvation is settled – not by works but by faith – so we keep the commandments not to earn salvation but to please him who has saved us. Justification, rightly understood, will make us grateful, assured, joyful obedient Christians.

Homework

- 1. What does God require of us before he will accept us?
- 2. Define justification
- 3. What are the two sides of justification?
- 4. Show how the law makes a double demand (negative and positive) upon its subjects. Illustrate from the eighth commandment – 'You shall not steal.'
- 5. For what reasons did Jesus need to be perfect?
- 6. What is the basis of our justification?
- 7. When is a person justified?
- 8. How is the doctrine of justification helpful to the Christian?

7

A New Family – Adoption

We might think that being accounted righteous in God's sight would be the most wonderful position we could come to in this life: but that is not so. J. I. Packer in his excellent book *Knowing God* maintains, rightly I believe, that adoption is the highest privilege the gospel offers. It is not the most essential blessing – justification takes that position, but adoption is the most precious of the many blessings given to us in Christ. In justification, God deals with us as our Judge: in adoption he deals with us as our Father. Justification gives us a right standing with God: adoption brings us into the family of God. Note the following references: 'Yet to all who received him [Christ], to those who believe in his name, he gave the right to become children of God –' (John 1:12). 'You are all sons of God through faith in Christ Jesus' (Gal. 3:26).

Note that both verses speak of faith. As we are justified by faith, so we also become God's children by faith. That doesn't mean they happen at different times. When we believe in the Lord Jesus Christ we are justified and adopted at the same time. We cannot be justified without being adopted, and we cannot be adopted without being justified.

There are two ways of entering a family: by birth and by adoption. Both concepts are used in the New Testament. Every Christian is born into God's family and also adopted, but each has certain characteristics that the biblical writers employ. When we are born into a family we have the life of our parents. Although distinct individuals, we inherit many of their traits: there is a likeness to our parents. So, when we are born into God's family, we possess divine life and there is a likeness to our heavenly Father (1 John 2:29). When someone is adopted into a family, they enter a family that they were not born into. They are adopted by a deliberate choice of the parents and assume a place in a family in which they formerly had no part. We were born in Adam's race. Indeed the Bible paints a worse picture – we were children of the devil (John 8:44, 1 John 3:10). By a deliberate, gracious act, God chose us to be his children and adopted us into his family.

When we talk of adoption today, we usually think of a couple adopting a baby or young child. Sometimes people adopt older children, but that is not nearly so common. In New Testament times adoption was quite different. Almost always it involved older teenagers or adults, generally males, and it was to meet the need of the one who did the adopting. It was a matter of inheritance. A man of standing might find himself in the position of having no heir, so he would adopt a young man to become his heir. This is the concept of adoption that Paul often spoke of, as for example in Galatians 4: 'But when the time had fully come, God sent his Son, born of a woman, born under the law, to redeem those under the law, that we might receive the full rights [or adoption] of sons...and since you are a son, God has made you also an heir' (Gal. 4:4-7).

Usually when Paul spoke of adoption he referred to believers as 'sons'. That term does not exclude women, but it conforms to the idea already mentioned. Adoption at that time involved taking a son rather than a daughter, and it was for the purpose of becoming an heir.

Imagine the reaction of a young man who is born into poverty, but who suddenly finds himself the heir of a wealthy man! That gives some idea of the privilege of sonship. John gets quite excited about this concept when he writes: 'How great is the love the Father has lavished on us, that we should be called children of God!...' (1 John 3:1). John is probably thinking of birth into God's family rather than adoption, but the end result is the same. God has lavished his love on us and made us his children. That ought to get us excited.

The doctrine of adoption follows similar lines to that of justification in that it is received by faith and also grounded in the work of Christ. We could also add that it has its roots in God's electing grace: '...In love he predestined us to be adopted as his sons through Jesus Christ...'(Eph. 1:4,5). Because of this similarity, most older books written on the subject of adoption simply viewed it as an aspect of justification. However, this does not do justice to the wonder of this truth, and it deserves separate treatment.

The Fatherhood of God

God's position as Father is treated in four different ways in the Bible.

- **1. He was the Father of Israel.** The prophet Hosea wrote: 'When Israel was a child, I loved him, and out of Egypt I called my son' (Hosea 11:1). This passage was quoted by Matthew as applying to Jesus after he was taken to Egypt as a baby (Matthew 2:13-15), but there is no doubt that it was also applied to the nation of Israel (see Exodus 4:22,23). God fathered the nation in the sense that he brought it into being.
- **2. He is the Father of the Lord Jesus Christ.** This hardly needs enlarging upon. Jesus was God's Son in a very unique sense: that is why he is called God's 'one and only Son' or 'only begotten Son' (KJV).

• **3. He is the Father of all people by creation.** When Paul was preaching in Athens he said: 'For in him we live and move and have our being. As some of your own poets have said, "We are his offspring"' (Acts 17:28). This Fatherhood is only in the context of creation. The vast majority of references to his Fatherhood are in the redemptive sense, so:

• **4. He is the Father of all who believe in Jesus Christ.** 'You are all sons of God through faith in Christ Jesus' (Galatians 3:26). God's Fatherhood in this sense is really a New Covenant blessing. Although as we have mentioned, the nation of Israel was seen as God's son (see also Isaiah 63:16), there are very few references to individuals being God's sons. Most of these are prophetic (2 Sam. 7:14) or used as a simile (Ps. 103:13). No individual in the Old Testament ever addressed God as his or her Father. Adoption is a New Covenant blessing. J. I. Packer wrote:

> For everything that Christ taught, everything that makes the New Testament new, and better than the Old, everything that is distinctively Christian as opposed to merely Jewish, is summed up in the knowledge of the Fatherhood of God. 'Father' is the Christian name for God (*Knowing God*).

The Old Testament name for God was 'Yahweh' (Jehovah). The name by which we come to God is 'Father'. Jesus laid the foundation for this in his earthly ministry. In the Sermon on the Mount he spoke often of God as the Father of his disciples, those in his kingdom (Matt. 5:16, 6:1,4,6,8 etc.), but this only came to full fruition after Jesus' resurrection. After he rose from the dead, Jesus sent Mary Magdalene to the disciples with a wonderful message: '...Go...to my brothers and tell them, "I am returning to my Father and your Father, to my God and your God"' (John 20:17). From that time on God would be their Father in a special and new way.

The permanence of adoption

Once more there is the parallel to justification. If we are children of God now, we will always be his children. We may disappoint him, we may grieve him, but we will never be cast out of his family or disinherited.

It is sometimes said that people raised in a family where the father was a bad lot, cannot appreciate the concept of the Fatherhood of God, because they will always have a negative view of fatherhood. But that is surely faulty reasoning. However bad a father may have been, no one will claim that all fathers are as bad as their own. They must have had friends or seen other families where the father was loving, faithful and a good provider; and doubtless they would have longed for a father like that. To have experienced only a bad father would make a good father very attractive. My own father left my mother and I for another woman when I was only seven. To know that God is not like that and that his family is stable and secure is a most attractive concept. God is a good Father: he is a perfect Father. As already mentioned we will explore the security of the believer in a later chapter.

The assurance of being God's children

Continuing the parallel between justification and adoption, we can be assured that we are children of God. All the promises that assure us that we are forgiven and right with God, will also give us the confidence that we are his children. This assurance is important because the devil will often try to make us doubt God's love. He is called 'the accuser of the brothers', accusing us before God day and night (Rev. 12:10). When we sin, he will make the accusation that we are not worthy to be God's children because of our failures. We need the reminder that God will never cease to love us: his is an everlasting love (Jer. 31:3), and that we can never cease to be his children.

In addition to the promises giving us assurance we also have the Holy Spirit's witness that we are God's children: 'For you did not receive a spirit that makes you a slave again to fear, but you received the Spirit of sonship. And by him we cry, "Abba, Father". The Spirit himself testifies with our spirit that we are God's children' (Rom. 8:15,16). This witness is something that no human being can give us, and no human being can take from us. It is a precious inward witness that we are indeed children of God.

The inheritance

As already noted, the purpose of first century adoption was to provide an heir for the person adopting, and we are said to be heirs of God. Note the following passages: 'Now if we are children, then we are heirs – heirs of God and co-heirs with Christ…' (Rom. 8:17). 'Because you are sons, God sent the Spirit of his Son into our hearts, the Spirit who calls out, "Abba, Father". So you are no longer a slave, but a son; and since you are a son, God has made you also an heir' (Gal. 4:6,7).

What is the inheritance? Normally we think of an inheritance involving material things – money, goods or property, but the inheritance that believers will come into is of a different kind. It can never perish spoil or fade, for it is in heaven (1 Peter 1:4). Many things are said to be our inheritance: ***eternal life*** (Matthew 19:29), ***the earth*** – presumably the new earth (Matthew 5:5), ***salvation*** – future salvation (Heb. 1:14), ***God's kingdom*** (James 2:5). We might say it is all the glory of the world to come and God's eternal kingdom. Another way to look at it is to see Christ's inheritance. He is said to be 'heir of all things' (Hebrews 1:2), and as we are described as co-heirs with Christ we shall inherit 'all things'. This is too much for us to grasp in this life. Paul wrote, quoting from Isaiah: '"No eye has seen, no ear has heard, no mind has conceived what God has prepared for those who love him"' – but God has revealed it to us by his Spirit' (1 Cor. 2:9,10).

We may have some inkling of our inheritance as we read a book like Revelation, but what is written there is often in symbolic terms and is hard to understand. Enough is revealed to encourage and spur us on, but much is left unsaid. We don't need to know all about heaven in this life. All we can say is that it will be wonderful, and we should indeed long for it. More will be said about this in the final chapter.

The practical effects of adoption

Adoption is not only designed to encourage us to look ahead to the world to come, but it should have a profound effect upon our behaviour in this life. To put this in the form of a question: What does adoption do for us here and now?

It gives us access to God

As already noted, being justified gives us a right standing with God as our Judge, but adoption gives us access to God as our Father. This is a high privilege indeed! In this world it is almost impossible to gain access to a monarch. In one of my pastorates, a teenage girl in our church heard that the Queen was coming to Canada and would be passing through our town. She wrote to her majesty and asked if she would stop in for tea on her way through. She received a nice reply, thanking her for the invitation, but saying that this was not possible. An ordinary citizen could not hold out much hope of getting access to the Queen. But if I were the Queen's son, that would be a very different story. Just as a son expects access to his parents so we have free access into the presence of our heavenly Father. We don't need an appointment to come before him: 24 hours a day his throne is accessible. Do we avail ourselves of this great privilege? How much time do we spend in prayer? We ought to be often at the throne of grace.

Some Christians never seem to address God as Father. This is not the only correct way to address him, but if adoption gives us the highest blessing as believers, then we should think of him mostly as our Father, and address him as such. One can only conclude that those who never address God as Father have never been gripped by the wonder of our adoption as God's children.

Adoption means that we are cared for by God

A good father will work hard to provide for his family, and the children expect that a home, food and clothing will always be there for them. There are, of course, some homes where this does not happen. Poverty and tragedy can bring great hardships to a family, but our heavenly Father is never hindered in his providing for his children. He is a good Father and has all the means at his disposal to care for his children. Paul assured the Philippian Christians: '...My God will meet all your needs according to his glorious riches in Christ Jesus' (Phil. 4:19). As has often been pointed out, wants and needs are not the same thing; and God's perception of our needs may be very different from ours, but God will provide for what he sees as our needs for as long as he sees fit. It is a wonderful promise that we may rest upon.

Adoption means that we are directed by God

Guidance is a big topic in itself. Simply put it means that God our Father shows us the way in which we should walk. A good earthly father in caring for his children is not content just to put a roof over their heads, and food on their table; he is concerned that they live productive lives and he will see that they are educated and taught how to live within society.

When the nation of Israel left Egypt and went into the desert, a pillar of cloud guided them by day and a pillar of fire by night. Sometimes as Christians we wish that guidance was that straightforward for us. However we must not imagine that our Father in heaven is less concerned to guide us than he was to guide Israel. The Lord Jesus Christ is described as the 'Good Shepherd' (John 10:11). A shepherd wants the sheep to know the way they should go, and our Good Shepherd wants us, his spiritual sheep, to know the way we should go. With a heavenly Father and a Good Shepherd to guide us, knowing God's will should not be hard. One of our problems is that we want God to give us a personalized blueprint for our lives, but that is not the way God usually guides us. There may be times when circumstances direct our way, as for example when an accident puts us in hospital. There are occasions when a powerful inward conviction orders our steps, as when Paul was prevented from entering Bithynia (Acts 16:7), but normally God directs us by his Word – the Bible. Certainly that is where we are to seek guidance.

Often in seeking God's guidance we ask the wrong question. We pray, 'Lord, show me your plan for my life', whereas we should be asking, 'Lord, show me the kind of life you want me to live.' Seeking God's will for our own life can be selfish. Our main concern should be to live in a way that pleases and glorifies God. When we think more along these lines, we will see that God's plan for our lives is laid out in Scripture – not in an individualized road map, but in principles by which we should live. When we take that approach, we can be sure of knowing God's will for the general activities of our life; where we do need specific direction, such as in seeking a job, our heavenly Father will provide that in some way or other. As his children we may have confidence in that.

The responsibilities of sonship

No privileged position is without responsibilities, and our position as God's children, blessed and privileged as it is, does carry certain responsibilities. This is true in an earthly family. There is the family honour to maintain. If a boy is playing with his friends and one of them insults his father, he will defend him fiercely. When children misbehave, their actions reflect on the whole family and if serious, bring disgrace on the parents. The same applies in our relationship with God. Let us note two areas of responsibility as children of God.

We must be like our Father

We spoke earlier about a child's likeness to his parents. My son Stephen is very like me, not only in appearance but also in mannerisms and personality. People say, 'He is very like his father.' As children of God, we should be very like our heavenly Father. This likeness is not physical but spiritual; nevertheless we should be like him. This is one of the themes in the Sermon on the Mount. Jesus said: 'You have heard that it was said, "Love your neighbour and hate your enemy". But I tell you: Love your enemies and pray for those who persecute you, that you may be sons of your Father in heaven' (Matt. 5:43-45).

Loving our enemies will show that we are children of God. It is not natural to love your enemies, and those who do so show that they have God's help and character is doing that. A little later, he added: 'Be perfect, therefore, as your heavenly Father is perfect' (Matt. 5:48).

Our immediate response to such a statement will probably be, 'Impossible! How can we be perfect?' We can't in this life, but our goal will always be perfection (Paul in 2 Cor. 13:11 says, '...aim for perfection...'), however the standard will not just be a list of moral commands, but likeness to our Father or the Lord Jesus Christ himself. That is the mark of our sonship. The apostle John has much to say on this subject. Speaking of God and his children he writes: 'If you know that he is righteous, you know that everyone who does what is right has been born of him' (1 John 2:29). For John, the proof of being God's children is not in any profession but giving evidence of the fact by being like our Father. John goes further, saying that you can tell the difference between God's children and the devil's: 'Dear children, do not let anyone lead you astray. He who does what is right is righteous, just as he is righteous. He who does what is sinful is of the devil...' (1 John 3:7,8). A few verses later, after proceeding along the same line, John adds: 'This is how we know who the children of God are and who the children of the devil are...' (verse 10).

We may not always be able to distinguish at a given moment, but in the long run you can tell the difference. God's children are like their Father – not perfectly like him, but sufficiently like him to distinguish them from the devil's children. Our concern and prayer should be that this likeness be evident to those who know us – our family, our friends, our workmates, our neighbours.

We should love our brothers and sisters in Christ

It is a well known saying that 'blood is thicker than water'. Every family has its squabbles, but when there is a threat from outside the family, they will usually stand together. As we have just seen we are to love even our enemies; that takes grace, but we are particularly called upon to love our fellow-christians because they are our brothers and sisters in Christ. Jesus said to his disciples: 'A new commandment I give you: Love one another. As I have loved you, so you must love one another. By this all men will know that you are my disciples, if you love one another' (John 13:34,35).

Loving others wasn't the new command. The law required the people to love their neighbour as themselves (Lev. 19:18). What was new was the new relationship that believers had with one another as children of God, and of course the standard – loving as Christ loved. Most of us have seen church quarrels, often with people leaving a church because they couldn't get along with other Christians. Not only is this sad, but it is a poor witness to the world in which we live. We need to show the world that we love our fellow-believers. This love was proverbial in the early church. It was said of them by their persecutors: 'Behold how these Christians love one another.' O that people might say that of us today! John takes this a little further: 'We know that we have passed from death to life, because we love our brothers...' (1 John 3:14).

Not only are we commanded to love our brothers: not only is our love a powerful witness to the world, but that love is an evidence that we are God's children: that we are born again. John puts this in even stronger terms: 'Anyone who hates his brother is a murderer, and you know that no murderer has eternal life in him' (1 John 3:15). Jesus had taught that hatred was murder (Matt. 5:21,22); John is applying it to professing Christians. Both murder and hatred can be forgiven, but an ongoing hatred towards God's children is an indication that the person knows nothing of eternal life.

We have to be honest and admit that some Christians are very hard to love. If we are even more honest and take a good look at ourselves, we may be amazed that anyone could love us. We all have our defects, and while conversion brings about a radical change, it does not alter our basic personality. As it is sometimes hard to love other Christians, so it must be equally hard for them to love us. How can we love the unlovely? We are particularly thinking of Christians here. We need to see them as children of God for God has loved them as he has loved us, and he has brought us all into his family. If there are some aspects of their characters that are not nice, think what they must have been like before. The same Spirit of God who indwells us, indwells them too. When we marvel at God's grace in ourselves and others, we will find it a lot easier to love all God's children.

The responsibilities of being children of God are far-reaching, but they shouldn't discourage us. It is a marvellous thing to be part of God's family. It is a privilege to know others who are God's children. It is humbling to be in a community where people lavish love upon us even when they hardly know us. We often experience more love and care from our spiritual family than from our natural family, because the bonds of love in Christ exceed any natural bonds. We need to keep focussed on the blessedness of our position. We can do no better than conclude this chapter by repeating John's words: 'How great is the love the Father has lavished on us that we should be called children of God! And that is what we are…!'(1 John 3:1)

Homework

- 1. What are the two ways of entering a family?
- 2. Show how both these ways are used to illustrate how a person enters God's family.
- 3. In what sense can it be said that God is the Father of everyone?
- 4. Can everyone legitimately pray the Lord's prayer (Matt. 6:9-13)?
- 5. Compare the blessings of adoption with those of justification.
- 6. What is the inheritance of God's children?
- 7. Why would some Christians not address God as 'Father'?
- 8. Why is a holy lifestyle important for God's children?
- 9. How can the doctrine of adoption help us when we find it hard to love some Christians?

8

Holy Living – Sanctification

In the last two chapters we have been considering what happens when people are converted. They are justified, that is, declared righteous by God; and they are also adopted into God's family and called children of God. These are rich blessings, wonderful privileges that make the Christian ready for heaven. But the fact is that usually people do not go to heaven as soon as they are converted. Most are converted in their teens but even when we take into account those converted later in life, the average age will still not be far from twenty; which means that most believers spend more than half a century in this world as Christians. It goes without saying then that the way we spend that time is very important.

God's plan of salvation deals with the problem of sin. When we believe in the Lord Jesus Christ, our sins are forgiven: they are no longer counted against us. However, sin does not disappear at this point. Many a Christian in the euphoria of conversion has imagined that he or she has done with sin forever. What a rude awakening it is when we find that sin is still very much a part of our life! We saw in the last chapter that we are told to 'aim for perfection' (2 Cor. 13:11), but alas, however good our intentions are, we don't achieve perfection in this life: we still sin. So where does that leave us?

We have said that when we are justified, God sees us without sin, and yet we do sin, and God knows we sin. Does this sound confusing? How can he see us without sin when in fact we do sin? At this point we need to understand an important theological distinction. We need to see the difference between justification and sanctification. We have already defined justification but it is worth repeating: justification is God pardoning the sinner and declaring him righteous. The key word there is 'declaring'. When we are justified we are not righteous, but are declared righteous. God's righteousness in Christ is imputed to us. Sometimes the Bible uses the picture of a garment being put upon us. In Zechariah 3:1-5 we have the picture of Joshua the high priest of Israel standing before God in filthy clothes. The command is given to remove his old clothes and to clothe him with clean garments. It is a picture of God's people having their sins forgiven and then being seen as righteous. The clothes of most people in the Middle East to this day are long and cover almost all the body. Only the face shows. When you look at someone you see little but clothes, so a long robe is a good picture of justification. When we are justified we are initially no different in our lives, but God sees us as righteous. Paul says that God 'justifies the wicked' (Rom. 4:5). He means that at the point of conversion we are still wicked. We have been convicted of our sin, and come to God with the intention to forsake sin, but at that moment we are still sinful. However, from that point on there is an inward change and there begins a life-long battle with sin: a process of becoming holy. This is sanctification. *The Westminster Shorter Catechism* defines sanctification:

> Sanctification is the work of God's Spirit, whereby we are renewed in the whole man after the image of God, and are enabled more and more to die unto sin, and live unto righteousness (Question 34).

Notice the 'more and more'. Sanctification is a process,

beginning at conversion and ending in glory. God's work of justification is instantaneous, whereas his work of sanctification is life long. The words sanctify, sanctuary, sanctification and holy all come from the same root in the biblical languages. The word 'holy' literally means 'set apart' or different. It was originally used of material things, for example in connection with the Jewish tabernacle. Certain rooms, utensils or items of furniture, were holy. They were set apart for special use. Some pots and pans were used for cooking meat from the sacrifices. They were set apart for such use, and it would be unthinkable for the wife of a priest to borrow one of these pots to cook dinner for her family.

The word 'holy' was often used to describe the Lord himself: 'Exalt the LORD our God and worship at his footstool; he is holy. (Ps. 99:5). God is set apart from all other beings. He is different. Gradually the word assumed an ethical character. God's people were to be holy. They were to be different, and that difference had to be seen in their righteous lives. Sanctification then is the life-long process of becoming more holy; more like Christ.

The difference between justification and sanctification is an important one. Both are the work of God, and both are a part of God's work of saving us from our sins. However, there are important distinctions. Justification is something done for us; sanctification is something done in us. Justification is a once-for-all declaration by God; sanctification is an ongoing, inward work of God. Our justification can never be improved upon, because we are seen perfect in Christ; our sanctification is constantly being improved upon, because we are never actually perfect in this life. Justification alone gives us the right to enter heaven; sanctification makes us fit to enter heaven.

This last point is particularly important because many Christians base their assurance of salvation upon their day-to-day behaviour. Imagine a day in Mary's life: she wakes up in good time feeling fresh. After washing and getting dressed, she spends an hour in prayer and Bible reading. The Lord seems very near. She goes to work feeling the glow of sweet fellowship with the Lord. Things go well in the office: her boss is in a good mood and says how pleased she is with Mary's work. That day Mary completes all her assignments well and in good time. Over lunch she has a wonderful opportunity to speak to a colleague about the things of God. The woman even promises to come to church with her next Sunday. In the evening she visits an old lady in a nursing home and while there she is able to talk to several of the residents, and in particular to cheer up an old man who seemed so despondent when she arrived. As she prays before going to bed, her heart is full of gratitude to the Lord and she praises him for her salvation and for the joy of being a child of God.

Now see Mary a week later. She doesn't sleep well most of the night, then falls into a deep sleep just before it is time to get up. She doesn't hear the alarm and wakes up late with a terrible headache. She has no time for devotions or for breakfast. At work her boss seems to be growling at everyone and at Mary in particular. She makes all kinds of mistakes in her typing, and the boss shouts at her for a big mistake in one document. Before the day is out, she loses her temper with the same colleague she had witnessed to last week. That evening Mary's sister comes to see her and they get into a big argument about some family matter. When Mary kneels beside her bed that night she is broken hearted and can't believe that she can be a Christian.

What a difference a week makes! What went wrong? Nobody is going to make excuses for her bad behaviour, and we have already noted that we do need to confess our sins to the Lord. We also noted that assurance is tied in part to our obedience to the Lord, but Mary and many other believers, tie assurance entirely to behaviour: when they have a good day, they have assurance of salvation, and when they have a bad day, they lose that assurance. We all have good and bad days – again, no excuse for the bad days, but does our acceptance with God depend upon a good day? Of course not; it depends on the work of Christ, and as far as we are concerned, it depends on our justification not our sanctification. God does not stop loving us when we sin. We may lose the sense of his presence, and we need to confess our sins, but we must look to Christ and the cross for our hope and confidence.

Having said that, our behaviour is very important, and the process of becoming more holy is a very large part of the Christian life. We will examine several aspects of sanctification.

The necessity of sanctification

There are many passages of Scripture that make this clear. Note the following: 'Make every effort to live in peace with all men and to be holy; without holiness no one will see the Lord' (Heb. 12:14). 'What good is it, my brothers, if a man claims to have faith but has no deeds? Can such faith save him? Suppose a brother or sister is without clothes and daily food. If one of you says to him, "Go, I wish you well; keep warm and well fed," but does nothing about his physical needs, what good is it? In the same way, faith by itself, if it is not accompanied by action, is dead' (James 2:14-17).

The KJV rendering of this last passage has more punch: 'Faith without works is dead.' This necessity is not for the purpose of earning salvation: we have already established that salvation is by grace, not works.

There have been some people in the history of the church who have taught that as salvation is by grace, and does not depend upon works, it does not matter how we live. We are going to heaven anyway, so the time between conversion and death is irrelevant. That is simply not true. Let us look at some of the reasons why sanctification or holiness is not only important – it is essential in the believer.

Holiness glorifies God

This is something often overlooked in Christian circles. Note Paul's words to the Ephesians: 'In him we were also chosen, having been predestined according to the plan of him who works out everything in conformity with the purpose of his will, in order that we, who were the first to hope in Christ, might be for the praise of his glory' (Eph. 1:11,12).

Salvation is not primarily for our benefit, but for God's glory. If we who profess faith in Christ behave like the people of the world, then it is not surprising that those who observe us will be turned off. When trying to tell people about Christ, how often have we heard it said: 'The church is full of hypocrites!' The person we are talking to may work alongside a professing Christian and have seen many inconsistencies in his or her life. We also hear too often, 'If that's Christianity, I don't want it!' So God is dishonoured and the gospel is discredited when those who claim to follow Christ do not follow in the Master's footsteps.

Holiness proves the reality of our faith

On an earthly level there is no other way in which faith can be demonstrated. People profess to become Christians. It may be that they have a highly emotional experience, but that is possible without true faith. The parable of the sower (Matt. 13:1-23) teaches us that some people may receive the gospel with joy, and for a time may seem to live like true believers, but in time they fall away and lose interest. The test of a true work of God's grace is perseverance in the faith: this will be looked at in the next chapter. The importance is not just so we will have an influence on others; it is the proof of our faith. There are many scriptural passages that stress the importance of continuing in the faith: let us look at a few. Jesus said: '…If you hold to my teaching, you are really my disciples' (John 8:31). 'My sheep listen to my voice; I know them, and they follow me' (John 10:27).

I remember as a young believer discussing this last verse with another Christian, and he said bluntly, 'There are some of Christ's sheep who don't follow him.' His words were certainly at variance with Jesus' statement. Paul wrote: 'For sin shall not be your master, because you are not under law, but under grace' (Rom. 6:14).

The apostle doesn't say that sin 'should not' be our master, but that it 'shall not' be our master. As already noted, we will never be perfect in this life, but once we become Christians we will not be mastered by sin. John follows the same line: 'No one who is born of God will continue to sin, because God's seed remains in him; he cannot go on sinning, because he has been born of God' (1 John 3:9. See also verse 6). Of course John is not saying that a Christian will never sin again after becoming a child of God. He has said earlier that 'If we claim to be without sin, we deceive ourselves…' (1 John 1:8). 'Continue to sin' means deliberately to continue in a path of known sin. No true believer does that.

No matter how loudly we profess to be Christians, our profession is nullified by unholy living. Jesus and the apostles are united in insisting on holiness of life for the disciples of the Lord. This is important for several reasons. It gives a measure by which unbelievers can assess the genuineness of Christianity – they will do that anyway. It gives the Christian a measure to assess his or her own faith – in conjunction with God's promises and the witness of the Spirit, remember. It is also a measure for Christians to assess each other. We ought not to go around constantly analysing other Christians, but there are times when it is helpful to know where a person stands. For example, when people apply for membership in a church, there has to be some means of assessing where they stand. Most churches known as 'evangelical', that is, committed to the Bible as God's inspired Word and to the truths of the gospel as the only way of salvation, only receive as members those who give evidence of being converted. The applicants will usually be interviewed by the officers of the church, who will not only want to know what they believe, but also to see some evidence that they behave as Christians.

Holiness or sanctification is a preparation for glory

At this point it is better to think of the lifetime process of sanctification rather than a state of holiness, because the whole of the Christian life is a preparation for the world to come. We have already stated that when a person is justified they are ready for heaven because God sees them as sinless in Christ. However, the fact is, that apart from a few, like the thief who died on the cross beside Jesus, most people do not go to heaven as soon as they are converted. There are different reasons for this. People have responsibilities towards family and others, although God does sometimes sees fit to remove a bread-winner from a family, leaving behind great hardship. Such events are his business not ours, but as a rule there is work for the believer to do in making known the gospel to others, and in serving the Lord in different ways. Another reason why most Christians stay in this world for a good many years is that God uses this time to prepare his children for glory. God's purpose for us in salvation is to conform us to his Son (Rom. 8:29). While we are on earth the essential moulding of our character is taking place but as we have already seen, the process is never completed in this life. The glorious truth is that at death all sin will be removed, and in the resurrection we will have new bodies that will never sin. But while we wait for heaven our characters are being formed here on earth.

In a number of places in the New Testament, the Christian life is likened to a race. The writer to the Hebrews urged his readers to: '...run with perseverance the race marked out for us' (Heb. 12:1). Speaking about the perfection at which he aimed, Paul said: 'Brothers, I do not consider myself yet to have taken hold of it. But one thing I do: Forgetting what is behind and straining toward what is ahead, I press on towards the goal to win the prize for which God has called me heavenward in Christ Jesus' (Phil. 3:13,14).

This is the language of one engaged in a race. Paul was the runner: he had a course marked out for him: he was straining to get the prize which was heaven. Near the end of his life he could say, '...I have finished the race...' (2 Tim. 4:7). Every Christian is in that race. We are pursuing a course throughout our life, and the measure of progress is not how many days or years we have lived, but how much progress we have made in Christ-likeness. Thank God, we shall be perfectly like Christ in heaven, but the process goes on throughout our earthly life.

Holiness prepares us for the judgement

We shall develop this more in the next chapter, but it is appropriate to mention it here. While our hope of heaven rests entirely on the work of Christ, and salvation is wholly of grace, still the Bible consistently teaches that the judgement will be by works. Not that God needs the judgement to find out whether or not we are truly saved, but at that time he will demonstrate to men and angels that his people can be identified by their works or character. In that day there will be some who hope to gain access to heaven because of their religious service. Jesus said: 'Not everyone who says to me, "Lord, Lord" will enter the kingdom of heaven, but only he who does the will of my Father who is in heaven. Many will say to me on that day, "Lord, Lord, did we not prophesy in your name, and in your name drive out demons and perform many miracles?" Then I will tell them plainly, "I never knew you. Away from me, you evildoers!"' (Matt. 7:21-23).

The criterion will not be religious activities but holiness. The people described were preachers and miracle workers, but at the same time they were 'evildoers'. In the terrible day when all people will stand before God and give account of their lives, religious profession will not be the deciding factor as to whether we are accepted into heaven, but rather holiness of life and faithful following of Jesus Christ.

The devil will try to make us stumble at every point, so we must remind ourselves again that while holiness of life will prove the genuineness of our faith, we will not be accepted in the last day just because we are holy, but because we are in Christ and trusting only in his merits. Our holiness proves our right to heaven, but our holiness is not the basis of our right to heaven – Christ is. The two things are put together in Ephesians: 'For it is by grace you have been saved, through faith – and this not from yourselves, it is the gift of God – not by works, so that no one can boast. For we are God's workmanship, created in Christ Jesus to do good works, which God prepared in advance for us to do' (Eph. 2:8-10).

We are not saved *by* works, but are saved *to do* good works. As the Reformers, the church leaders of the sixteenth century, would say, 'Faith alone saves, but the faith that saves is not alone.' They reiterated what Paul stated in the verse quoted above: that faith rather than works saves us, but when that faith is genuine it will always be accompanied and demonstrated by works, that is by holiness of life.

The nature of sanctification

We need to get beyond definitions and ask how it actually works in the life of a believer. What happens to a person as they are being sanctified? We might make a comparison to a plane flight. I have crossed the Atlantic more than thirty times and I must confess I look forward to each trip with some excitement. Especially I enjoy the take off and landing, and always try to get a window seat to see as much as possible. The take off is exhilarating and the landing eagerly awaited either because of meeting loved ones I haven't seen for some time, or because of coming home after a time away. The flight in between take off and landing is just a matter of moving towards the destination and is generally quite ordinary.

The process of sanctification is a bit like that. Each end of it there is what we might term a crisis experience, and the rest of the life is a matter of steady progress. Let us look at the three phases.

The radical break with sin

When a person is regenerated (born again) that experience is only the beginning of the Christian life and the sanctification process. There is a long way for the new convert to go, and not until glory will he or she shed the last vestige of sin. We all know by experience that sin is an all too frequent problem for us and a source of shame as well. However, even in the newest believer there has been a radical change. As we have seen there is the new birth – the imparting of a new governing principle in the person: God indwells them by his Holy Spirit and there is a radical break with sin. This is part of repentance. When we come to Christ we turn from sin, maybe not fully, but at least wholeheartedly. This is expressed by Paul: 'Therefore, if anyone is in Christ, he is a new creation; the old has gone, the new has come!' (2 Cor. 5:17). Elsewhere Paul describes the believer as 'dead to sin', that is dead to its mastery (Rom. 6:1-14). As John Murray put it:

> ...There is a decisive and definitive breach with the power and service of sin in the case of everyone who has come under the control of the provisions of grace (Collected works, Vol.2,)

Theologians refer to this phase as 'definitive sanctification'. It does not deliver the Christian totally from sin, but it does break the power of sin in the life. It will not prevent a lifetime struggle with sin, but it will ensure that a true believer will not be permanently engulfed by the power of sin, even if there are times in our lives when we seem to go backwards in our battle with sin. In a boxing match the eventual winner will receive some hard blows: he may even be knocked to the floor on occasions, but he will emerge victorious at the last bell. So in the Christian life we will be hurt, knocked down a few times, bruised and bloodied, but by God's grace we shall be victorious at the last.

The continuing process of sanctification

As we have said, the initial break with sin's power is only the beginning, not the end: there is a life-long process of progressive sanctification. The key word here is 'progressive'. There are some who claim that sanctification is instantaneous, but this is contradicted by Scripture: 'The path of the righteous is like the first gleam of dawn, shining ever brighter till the full light of day' (Proverbs 4:18). This verse agrees with the Shorter Catechism:

> Sanctification is the work of God's Spirit, whereby we are renewed in the whole man after the image of God, and are enabled more and more to die unto sin, and live unto righteousness (Question 34.)

'More and more', not all at once. Two things go on at the same time: dying to sin and living to righteousness. A gardener knows that there is a never-ending process of pulling up weeds as well as planting flowers and vegetables. So in the Christian life there is the ongoing process of dealing with sin and growing in Christ-likeness.

The different ways in which the Christian life is presented in the Bible also suggest that sanctification is a process rather than an instantaneous experience:

There is the concept of growth: Peter admonished his readers to '...Grow in the grace and knowledge of our Lord and Saviour Jesus Christ...' (2 Peter 3:18). Whether we take the growth of plants or children; growth takes time. It may not always be steady. There are spurts and setbacks; plateaus and dips, but the overall pattern is onward and upward. We have all seen graphs representing the cost of living. There are ups and downs, sometimes quite sharp, but over a period of time there is increase: the graph climbs. The Christian life is similar.

There is the concept of maturity: In 1 John 2:13, John addresses three classes of believers, according to their spiritual maturity: fathers, young men and children. Maturity comes with time. Some mature quicker than others, but all of us have to grow from spiritual infancy to adulthood.

There is the concept of warfare: Paul urges Timothy to 'Fight the good fight of the faith...' (1 Tim. 6:12). There is a more extended treatment of spiritual warfare in Ephesians 6:10-18. Wars are not won overnight. Some battles are lost as well as won before the final victory is obtained. Once again, time is involved.

There is the concept of fruit bearing: As God's children we are to bear the 'fruit of the Spirit' – '...love, joy, peace etc...' (Gal. 5:22,23). Those who grow fruit know that they have to plant and water and prune and wait before they see fruit. There is a period of hard work and growth before harvest.

It would be wonderful and save us a lot of pain and groaning if we could be perfectly sanctified in a moment, but it is not to be. If we claim entire sanctification we will only deceive ourselves, and in the long run cause ourselves more pain. We have instant coffee, instant potatoes and instant dinners, but we cannot have instant sanctification: it takes time – a life-time.

The final deliverance: To return to the illustration of the plane flight – however long the journey seems, eventually the plane lands: it reaches its destination. This life will have its battles and heartaches; its joys and sorrows, but one day the journey will end – we shall 'land' in the celestial city. Either we shall die, or the Lord Jesus Christ will return, and we shall be with him forever. Then, and not till then, shall we be perfect: all sin will be gone, and as John says: '...We shall be like him...' (1 John 3:2).

The means of sanctification

We have seen the necessity and nature of sanctification. It remains to look at the means of sanctification. How does the process of conforming us to Christ actually take place?

We saw earlier that it is the work of God's Spirit. We must never imagine that sanctification is our work. It is a phase of God's work of grace to save us from our sins. Justification as we saw, is entirely God's work, but sanctification is different in that we are very much involved in it. We must work out our salvation (Phil. 2:12). While we cannot sanctify ourselves, yet at the same time we do not sit idly by and wait for God to work. We must be active in this. Indeed it is fair to say that sanctification is our responsibility. If we are not holy we have no one to blame but ourselves. As Churchill said at the beginning of World War II, 'Give us the tools and we will finish the job.' God has given us the tools, and by his grace we need to use them to finish the job of sanctification. What are the tools?

What are the means that God has given us for our sanctification? There are many:

The cross

This works in two ways:

First: we are said to be crucified with Christ. Not only did Christ die for his people, but his people died with him. Paul said, 'I have been crucified with Christ...' (Gal. 2:20). This ties in with being dead to sin, that is, dead to its power (see also Rom. 6:1-14).

Second: the cross is a powerful motivation to holiness. In many ways God's requirements for the believer are the same as for the Jews under the law, but the big difference is that we see God's love for us in Christ and are moved by that love to obey him. Jesus said, 'If you love me, you will obey what I command' (John 14:15). A mere list of rules will never motivate us to obedience, but when we consider the sacrifice of Christ at Calvary, we will surely want to please him who loved us and gave himself for us.

The Word of God

Jesus prayed for his disciples: 'Sanctify them by the truth; your word is truth' (John 17:17). The Word of God plays a large part in the sanctification of Christians. As we read it and meditate upon it, it purifies our thoughts and teaches us what is pleasing to God. As we listen to the preaching of the Word we are challenged to put it into practice. It is not hard to see how much we are responsible for our sanctification at this point, because we can read as much or little as we choose, and attend as many or as few meetings as we please. Not that reading the Bible or attending services automatically guarantees that we will be made more holy, but neglect of such means will guarantee that we will not be as holy as we might be. We need to obey what we read and hear to become more holy, but if we do not read or hear, then we have nothing to work with.

The Word is likened to food (Heb. 5:11-14, 1 Peter 2:2). If we don't eat and drink, we don't grow, and that is just as true in the spiritual realm as in the natural. We must give ourselves a steady diet of Scripture, and we must be careful of being too selective. We may have favourite passages to which we return again and again. That is fine, but we must remember that 'All Scripture is God-breathed and useful…' (2 Tim. 3:16). Some may be more useful than others. The letter to the Romans may be more helpful than the genealogies of Chronicles, but we must not neglect any of the Bible as it is inspired or God-breathed. When I was a young Christian I attended some Bible studies where the teacher once told us that one day we would be in heaven and would meet people like Hosea and Haggai. If they asked us how we enjoyed their books, it would be embarrassing to tell them we had never read them! It is a good practice to read systematically through the Bible so that we familiarize ourselves with all that God has moved his servants to write for our benefit.

The power of God

We can never be holy by practical means alone. We may read the Bible through once a month, but we cannot obey it without God's power. Thankfully, God's power is not only available to us, but given to us by the Holy Spirit. Actually the Father, Son and Holy Spirit are all said to indwell us (John 14:23, 1 Cor. 3:16). Every believer is indwelt by God and enabled to do what God wants us to do. Paul could say, 'I can do everything through him who gives me strength' (Phil. 4:13).

The ordinances

We are thinking of baptism and the Lord's Supper. Neither of these automatically convey grace, but rightly used they are most valuable. Baptism of course occurs but once in a believer's life. It is a step of obedience and a public declaration of a person's faith and of his intent to follow and obey Christ. It brings the person into the visible church, and is a time of great blessing and strength to the Christian.

The Lord's Supper is a commemoration of Christ's death and rightly approached will help and encourage God's people. Any consideration of Christ's death for us will both strengthen and motivate us to holiness.

Christian fellowship

Paul points out in 1 Corinthians 15:33 that '...Bad company corrupts good character'. Conversely good company produces good character. We are influenced by our friends, and when our friends are Christians they should be a help to our sanctification. I am not saying we should never have unbelieving friends, but when we befriend unbelievers, it should always be with a view to winning them to the Lord. Our close friends will be Christians: those we can help and those who can help us in our Christian walk.

When we attend church services, it is not just for worship, though that may be the main reason. It is always a joy to meet others of like faith and to encourage one another. Listen to the author of Hebrews: 'And let us consider how we may spur one another on towards love and good deeds. Let us not give up meeting together, as some are in the habit of doing, but let us encourage one another – and all the more as you see the Day approaching' (Heb. 10:25).

To converse with other believers is helpful. We can share

our joys and sorrows: we can pray for one another: we can give and receive helpful counsel. All this can take place at public meetings, but it can also take place on other occasions as we exercise hospitality and do things together with others. It is a wonderful thing to have Christian friends. They can keep us from many pitfalls: they can give helpful advice: they can also rebuke us at times – something we all need on occasions.

Experience

We all go through a wide variety of experiences, some pleasant and some very painful. We need to see the hand of God in all things – something we call providence. We also need to see that God uses all experiences for our good. One of the most quoted verses in the Bible is Romans 8:28: 'And we know that in all things God works for the good of those who love him, who have been called according to his purpose.'

Paul is not saying that all things are good in themselves, but that God uses even bad things for his glory and our good. We don't have any problem seeing good events as coming from the hand of God. A pay increase, the birth of a child or the recovery of someone from a serious illness – we can readily thank God for such things. But what about a car accident, a diagnosis of cancer or having an unmarried daughter who gets pregnant? Then it is much harder to see the hand of God. However, God may use such heartaches for our good even more than the pleasant times. Spurgeon once said:

> I venture to say that the greatest earthly blessing that God can give to any of us is health, *with the exception of sickness.* Sickness has frequently been of more use to the saints than health has... A sick wife, a newly-made grave, poverty, slander, sinking of spirit, might teach us lessons nowhere else to be learned so well. Trials drive us to the realities of religion (*The Full Harvest,* p.414; Banner Of Truth Trust).

Experience is not only a good teacher, but an effective sanctifier. The psalmist said: 'Before I was afflicted I went astray, but now I obey your word' (Ps. 119:67); and again, 'It was good for me to be afflicted so that I might learn your decrees' (Ps. 119:71). These verses tell us that everything in life, good and bad, contributes to our sanctification, and the more we are aware of this fact, the better for us. If we fight against providences, or complain about our experiences, we will lose out spiritually and could become bitter; but if we recognize all things as coming ultimately from the hand of a loving heavenly Father, it will help us to benefit from everything that happens to us.

Throughout this chapter we have been reminded that sanctification is God's work, yet at the same time it is something we are heartily involved in. A balanced view of this is necessary. Some view sanctification as something in which we are entirely passive. 'Let go and let God' is a favourite expression used by some Christians. There is some truth in this, but it is not the whole truth. We cannot be sanctified by ourselves: we need the power of God; yet at the same time we must see that God is not sanctified for us: we must be holy. The balance is well expressed by Paul: '…Continue to work out your salvation with fear and trembling, for it is God who works in you to will and to act according to his good purpose' (Phil. 2:12,13).

Sanctification can be viewed as a cooperative effort between God and the believer. We could never describe election or justification as a cooperative effort, but sanctification can certainly be seen in that way. It is God who sanctifies us through and through – in spirit, soul and body (1 Thess. 5:23), but we are the ones who must pursue holiness. May God help us to do that with all of our powers, relying on all of God's power!

Homework

- 1. Define sanctification.
- 2. List the differences between sanctification and justification.
- 3. How does our level of holiness affect our Christian testimony?
- 4. How can God judge us in the last day by our works, if we are saved by faith?
- 5. How would you answer someone who told you they were perfect?
- 6. How does the cross help us to be holy?
- 7. How much are we responsible for our sanctification?
- 8. How would you counsel a Christian who was bitter because their business had failed?

9

Keeping on – Perseverance

It was the 1952 Olympic Games in Helsinki; the final of the men's 5000 metres. As the leading group entered the last lap, the British runner Chris Chattaway surged into the lead and was still ahead entering the final bend. The British fans cheered loudly, anticipating a victory for their hero. Twenty-five seconds later the great Czech runner Emil Zatopek crossed the finishing line first, followed by a French and a German runner. Where was Chattaway? A widely circulated photograph showed the finish. It also showed in the background the red-headed Chattaway sprawled on the track after tripping. The medals were not awarded to those leading with half a lap to go – all that mattered was the placing at the finish.

There are a good many people who start races but never finish. That is also true in the Christian life, which is often likened to a race. Many of us know of people who seemed to start well in the Christian life, but later they lost all interest in spiritual matters – permanently. Even in the Bible there are records of several who started well but ended badly; people like King Saul or Paul's former helper, Demas, who deserted the apostle and returned to the world (2 Tim. 4:10). One could think too of Judas who, like the other apostles, must have preached the gospel and performed miracles, yet betrayed his Master and committed suicide.

What happened to these people? Were they true believers

who turned back and lost their salvation, or were they never really saved? We have to be honest and say that the former often seems to be true. Many of these people were so sincere: they were godly: they were perhaps even preachers of the gospel who saw many converted as a result of their ministry. It is hard to accept the fact that they never really knew the Lord. We need to give some thought to this, not only because there are sharp differences of opinion on the subject, but because some Christians live in fear of losing their salvation. Consider the following Scripture passages: 'And this is the will of him who sent me, that I shall lose none of all that he has given me, but raise them up at the last day. For my Father's will is that everyone who looks to the Son and believes in him shall have eternal life, and I will raise him up at the last day' (John 6:39,40). 'My sheep listen to my voice: I know them, and they follow me. I give them eternal life, and they shall never perish; no one can snatch them out of my hand. My Father who has given them to me, is greater than all; no one can snatch them out of my Father's hand' (John 10:27-29).

Both passages have several things in common: Jesus is speaking; he refers to the Father giving him certain people – his sheep; they have eternal life and he speaks of the security of those who have come to him. It is hard to put any other interpretation on these verses except that those who have truly come to Christ are eternally secure. Paul writes: 'For those God foreknew he also predestined to be conformed to the likeness of his Son, that he might be the firstborn among many brothers. And those he predestined, he also called; those he called, he also justified; those he justified, he also glorified' (Rom. 8:29,30).

This is an important passage, and ties in with the theme of this book: that there is purpose and continuity in God's plan to save sinners. Out of the mass of sinful humanity, God chose some for salvation. To redeem those chosen, the Lord Jesus Christ came into this world and died. To call those chosen and redeemed, the Holy Spirit convicted, enlightened and brought them to faith so that they might be justified and brought into God's family. Romans 8:29,30 does not cover all the stages, but it follows a similar route. It begins with ***foreknowledge*** – not, as we saw in chapter 2, simply a knowing of facts about people, but God's sovereign, loving knowledge that they would be his people. These people he also ***predestined*** to be like his Son. Notice it is the same group – 'those', no more; no less. The same people, no more; no less, were ***called***. Again, the same people, no more; no less, were ***justified***; and the same group, no more; no less, were ***glorified***. Paul might have added other things in the chain, such as sanctification, but so certain is the conclusion that he goes directly from justification to glorification. From foreknowledge to glorification there is no room for change within the group: no room for additions and no room for dropouts. So we must conclude that all who were truly elect, redeemed, called, brought to faith and justified, must be glorified. That is what Jesus said in the verses just quoted from John. If they came to him, then they would be raised up in the last day. We say, without hesitation, that those truly saved can never be lost.

Why then do some hold contrary views? There are many, including whole denominations, such as Methodists and the Salvation Army, who teach that a true believer can be lost. A person can be saved today and lose that salvation the next day. Why the different views at this point? One reason we have already mentioned:

Some seem to be genuinely saved then fall away

We have cited biblical examples, and many of you will think back to people known personally. Whilst in the army in Singapore I remember a man who professed faith soon after I did. We were at a Christian leave centre together when he was convicted of his sins and asked the Lord to save him. When we returned to the camp I was immediately sent away on an arms escort to Malaya. I was apprehensive about leaving him alone as I knew of no other Christians in our barracks, however, when I returned five days later, everyone in our barrack room was talking about his conversion. He was witnessing about his faith to everyone he met, and giving out gospel tracts to many. I was thrilled and rejoiced in what seemed clear evidence of his salvation. Sadly within a few weeks he had abandoned his faith saying he wanted to pursue a career in gambling: his goal before he professed faith. How heavy my heart was then! But that is not an unusual happening, and is one reason why some teach that we can lose our salvation. How do we answer this?

By noting that not everyone who professes to be converted is genuine. They may be sincere, but that is no guarantee of true faith. As we saw with the race, it is not enough to start, nor even to be running well part way through the race. The most important thing is the finish. Note Paul's words to the Colossians: 'Once you were alienated from God and were enemies in your minds because of your evil behaviour. But now he has reconciled you by Christ's physical body through death to present you holy in his sight, without blemish and free from accusation – if you continue in your faith, established and firm, not moved from the hope held out in the gospel…' (Col. 1:21-23). Similarly in Hebrews we read: 'But Christ is faithful as a son over God's house. And we are his house, if we hold on to our courage and the hope of which we boast' (Heb. 3:6). 'We have come to share in Christ if we hold firmly to the end the confidence we had at first' (Heb. 3:14).

Each of these passages contains an important 'if'. We will be presented before God; we are God's house; we have come to share in Christ; 'if' we keep on to the end. It is the same message all over again – it is not enough to begin: we must finish too.

Now at this point someone may be agreeing with my argument, but still assuming that the people spoken of in these verses were once true believers – but that cannot be. We have already quoted several verses that speak of the security of those who have been truly converted. Other verses speak about those who seemed to be Christians but were not. In a previous chapter we quoted Jesus' words near the end of the Sermon on the Mount: 'Not everyone who says to me, "Lord, Lord" will enter the kingdom of heaven, but only he who does the will of my Father who is in heaven. Many will say to me on that day, "Lord, Lord, did we not prophesy in your name, and in your name drive out demons and perform many miracles?" Then I will tell them plainly, "I never knew you. Away from me, you evildoers!"' (Matt. 7:21-23).

It appears that those referred to were professing Christians and even Christian ministers, but they were eventually proved false by their ungodly lives. Notice that Jesus does not say, 'I knew you once, but not any longer', but rather, 'I never knew you.' Despite the appearance at one point, they were never true Christians. The parable of the sower in Matthew 13 tells of four places where the seed was sown: on the path, on rocky ground, among thorns and on good ground. In the last three places the seed germinated, but only in the last was there fruit. When Jesus interprets the parable he shows that in some lives, like seed on rocky or thorny ground, God's Word seems to take root and show signs of life, but in the end there is no fruit and therefore no real salvation. However well they start, if troubles or worldly obsessions cause them to go back, there was never a true work of grace.

Scriptures that seem to teach that a believer can lose his salvation

Another reason why some are convinced that a real Christian

can subsequently be lost is that some passages of the Bible do appear to teach this. Here are three such quotations:

•**1.** Peter writes; 'If they have escaped the corruption of the world by knowing our Lord and Saviour Jesus Christ and are again entangled in it and overcome, they are worse off at the end than they were at the beginning. It would have been better for them not to have known the way of righteousness, than to have known it and then to turn their backs on the sacred command that was passed on to them. Of them the proverbs are true: "A dog returns to its vomit," and, "A sow that is washed goes back to her wallowing in the mud."' (2 Peter 2:20-22).

•**2.** 'My brothers, if one of you should wander from the truth and someone should bring him back, remember this: Whoever turns a sinner from the error of his way will save him from death and cover over a multitude of sins' (James 5:19,20).

•**3.** 'It is impossible for those who have once been enlightened, who have… tasted the goodness of the word of God and the powers of the coming age, if they fall away, to be brought back to repentance, because to their loss they are crucifying the Son of God all over again and subjecting him to public disgrace' (Heb. 6:4-6).

Certainly if someone read these verses and no others in the New Testament, they could be excused from concluding that it is indeed possible for a believer to lose his or her salvation. So how do we explain such passages in the light of the ones we have seen that clearly teach a Christian's salvation is secure? Obviously God knows the hearts of all, but the fact is that we have to deal with people whose hearts we do not know. We can only go by profession and evidence. That is why Scripture often views people in terms of their profession.

In the first passage Peter is writing about false teachers: those who had once professed faith in Christ and even been recognized as teachers in the church. However they later began to teach error, and eventually fell back into the kind of sinful lifestyle from which they seemed to have been delivered. Their 'knowing our Lord Jesus Christ' and their knowledge of the 'way of righteousness' was an intellectual knowledge only. The passage is teaching us that it is not enough to have a head knowledge of Christ and salvation – we need to believe in the heart as well (Rom. 10:9,10). From our standpoint, we never know the true state of people's hearts so all must be judged by appearance.

In the second passage from James, a backslider is restored and saved from death. If such a person was not restored, but continued in their sins, then they would not be rescued from death, proving that their faith was spurious.

The most difficult of the three passages quoted is the one from Hebrews. The people spoken of here had experienced something of the power of the gospel and the moving of the Holy Spirit in their hearts. It seems hard to believe that these were not real Christians, but as we read on in the same chapter, there are some words that help us to understand the passage. The writer says in verse 9, 'Even though we speak like this, dear friends, we are confident of better things in your case – things that accompany salvation.' The people being addressed were in great spiritual danger: they were turning back to the Old Covenant with its imposing temple, priesthood and ritual: they were in danger of leaving Christ, the '...mediator of a new covenant...' (Heb. 9:15) and returning to their old ways. The author does not specifically mention this danger in Hebrews 6 as he is persuaded of better things in their case: things that accompany salvation. Falling away from grace did not accompany salvation!

When the Bible seems to contradict itself, and says one thing in one place and another elsewhere, then we have to compare the passages carefully, for if the Scriptures are God-breathed (2 Tim. 3:16), they must be consistent. The problem then is not biblical contradictions but our lack of understanding. We are convinced that the salvation of a genuine believer is secure, not just because of a few proof texts, but because God is a sovereign God who plans and carries out his purposes. He planned to save some and bring them to glory, therefore nothing can frustrate his purposes, otherwise he is not God.

The value of the doctrine of perseverance

The obvious value is that of ***encouragement.*** When we are going through hard times or having doubts about our salvation, it is so encouraging to know that by God's grace we shall endure to the end. Some are more prone to doubts than others, and from a pastoral point of view they need more attention and help, but all of us at times get discouraged and wonder whether we will be able to hang on. When Chris Chattaway took the lead in that Olympic final, he hoped he could hang on to the end, but knew there was no certainty of it. He must have been feeling exhausted but knew that only his legs and no one else's could carry him to the finishing line. If we look at ourselves we must doubt whether we could ever endure to the end. But God has promised that with his help we shall reach the finishing line; we shall endure to the end. How that promise should fill us with great confidence! We have many such precious promises in Scripture and these will strengthen and motivate us to continue following Christ.

In Pilgrim's Progress, referred to earlier, the pilgrims were often given a sight of the celestial city in the distance to show them that their journey was not in vain. God is gracious and in his Word gives us many glimpses of heaven and the glory of the coming age. We need to consider these things so that we will not lose heart.

Some may ask whether the doctrine of perseverance might give some false assurance. It can if it is not held together with the other truths we have examined. The practice of some involved in mass evangelism can encourage a false assurance and hope. In a typical scene, the evangelist concludes his message with an appeal to those who want to accept Christ to come forward for counselling. Those who respond are often given assurance that they are God's children and heaven bound. I have met some of those who have been given that kind of assurance, and have later lost all interest in spiritual things, but who are still convinced that they will one day be in heaven. They can even quote some of the promises given to them when they responded to the evangelist's appeal. Clearly they have a false assurance, and need to be shown that their faith must be demonstrated by their godliness of life and love for the Lord. The promises of God have no validity for those not walking with the Lord, but for those who truly love Christ and seek to follow him, these promises are a precious comfort.

The doctrine of perseverance will also serve as a warning to us.

This doctrine is sometimes referred to as ***perseverance*** and sometimes as ***preservation***. The two designations give us the two sides of the doctrine. God will ***preserve*** his own people, but at the same time we must ***persevere***. We cannot rest upon the hope of preservation and assume that we need to do nothing. No, we must endure to the end. We must press on towards our goal, yet not in our own strength. These two things must be held in balance and both must be stressed. We noted that there are some very strong warnings in the book of Hebrews, and we have also seen several verses that contain the vital word 'if'. These passages are very practical. God promises that his people shall endure to the end, but that endurance is not without means, and one of the means is surely the warnings contained in God's Word. More is said about this in the next section.

The means of perseverance

God invariably uses means in carrying out his purposes, and the perseverance of his people is no exception. We looked at the means for our sanctification, and these will all apply to our perseverance, because perseverance is simply the carrying of sanctification through to its conclusion. There will of necessity be some overlap, but repetition is usually helpful.

God's promises

Several of these have been already been quoted, and there are many more. Job said, '…The righteous will hold to their ways…' (Job 17:9). Paul said he was '…Confident of this, that he who began a good work in you will carry it on to completion until the day of Christ Jesus' (Phil. 1:6). Peter wrote, 'And the God of all grace, who called you to his eternal glory in Christ, after you have suffered a little while, will himself restore you and make you strong, firm and steadfast' (1 Peter 5:10). These promises are food for the soul: they are refreshment along the Christian pathway: they will put a song in our hearts even when the going is rough.

God's warnings

William is halfway through the cross country race. He went too fast during the first mile and is now feeling exhausted and ready to drop out. The competitors are not only running for themselves but for the school. Eight need to finish to score for the team. Another boy in William's team is close to him and sees that he about to give up. He speaks sharply, 'If you drop out we won't be able to have a team result.' Those words spur William on and he manages to stagger to the finish to the cheers of his team-mates. His colleague might have given him words of encouragement, but sometimes warnings can be effective too. So it is in the Christian race. We may grow weary in the battle. We struggle with sin, and it often seems that it would be far easier to give in to temptation than resist it. At such times warnings can be helpful. They are means of grace, and just as the warnings of an earthly father can make us obedient when kind words don't, so there are times when our heavenly Father's warnings can smarten us up when more gentle means are not effective. When Paul wrote to the Galatian churches, he was deeply concerned because they were turning back to the ceremonies of the Jewish law. He said, 'I fear for you, that somehow I have wasted my efforts on you' (Gal. 4:11). What effect would his words have on them? Surely in the case of those who were genuine believers, his words would spur them on and make them determined to show Paul that his efforts had not been in vain.

Of course if we received nothing but warnings we should get very discouraged, and so in Scripture there is a balance between warnings and promises. We need both.

Discipline

In the church at Corinth there was a man guilty of immorality of the worst kind (1 Corinthians 5). Paul demands that the church excommunicate the man, but the reason is not just punitive – that is for a punishment, but corrective and restorative. Paul said: 'Hand this man over to Satan, so that the sinful nature may be destroyed and his spirit saved on the day of the Lord' (1 Cor. 5:5).

Some of what Paul says here is difficult to understand. 'Handing over to Satan', and the 'sinful nature being destroyed', have received many interpretations. However, we shouldn't let these difficulties take away from a very important point – the purpose of the church discipline was for his future good and salvation. The man had sinned greatly, but the excommunication could be the means of his restoration. Today, it is rarely exercised, but even if people are excommunicated from one church, they can often go round the corner to another church and be accepted with no questions asked. That wasn't so in the first century. There would be one church in Corinth and to be put out of the church would be a terrible experience for those who were, despite their sin, true believers. To be cut off from the means of grace and Christian fellowship would indeed be like being handed over to Satan, and was likely to bring about swift repentance. Discipline at any level, whether a rebuke or excommunication can be a wonderful means of grace for the wayward Christian and we should thank God for it.

The ministry of the Word

According to Jesus' prayer (John 17:17) we are sanctified by the truth which is God's Word. If we are to persevere to the end we must never neglect the Bible, either in private or in the public preaching and teaching of Scripture. David said, 'My heart is set on keeping your decrees to the very end' (Ps. 119:112). We never get beyond the learning stage because there is so much to learn from God's Word. One of the dangers of Christian maturity is in thinking that we know virtually all there is to know of the Bible, or at least that we know as much as we need to know. But God's Word keeps on sanctifying us and helps us to persevere. When we have been Christians for many years we will not often hear something that is completely new. We might often say or at least think, 'I've heard this before.' Perhaps we have, but we need to hear it again and again. How many times in the Bible do we get exhortations to prayer or to be pure or to be without covetousness? We need reminding of these things repeatedly, and we should never tire of hearing them and being reminded of them.

Sometimes we will hear a sermon and afterwards think we have not benefited because nothing in the message seemed to speak specially to us and nothing seemed new. Perhaps so but suppose you took a pebble from beside a stream and put it in the water. Six months later you return to examine it. What would you find? It would look pretty much the same as it did when you put it there, but at least it would be clean. The flowing water does not seem to change it, but it keeps it clean. If it had been left on the bank it would be dirty and perhaps moss would have grown on it, but that couldn't happen in the stream. The Word of God works in us in the same way. In a sermon there may not be anything that arrests our attention, but principles from Scripture we hear are helping to form our character and keep us pure. If we neglect the Bible or the public meetings of the church, this is far less likely to happen.

God's own power

Even if we have been diligent in using the various means of grace, we all still struggle and have times when we wonder if we can hang on in the Christian life. We need reminding over and over again that neither our sanctification nor our final perseverance is attained by our own efforts. Listen to what Peter said: 'Praise be to the God and Father of our Lord Jesus Christ! In his great mercy he has given us new birth into a living hope through the resurrection of Jesus Christ from the dead, and into an inheritance that can never spoil or fade – kept in heaven for you, who through faith are shielded by God's power until the coming of the salvation that is ready to be revealed in the last time' (1 Peter 1:3-5).

Through God's mercy we have new birth, we have an inheritance kept for us in heaven, and until we attain to that, we are kept or shielded by God's power. The word ***shielded*** means ***kept under guard.*** It is used of protective custody. A prisoner in jail is protected from escaping: we are protected from falling away. Our faith is vital: so also are our own efforts to continue following Christ, but in the last analysis it is God who keeps us and preserves us unto his heavenly kingdom. As Paul puts it, 'For it is God who works in you to will and to act according to his good purpose' (Phi. 2:13), yet we must 'Continue to work out our salvation with fear and trembling' (Phil. 2:12). Just as it is with sanctification, we are responsible to persevere to the end, yet we cannot do so without the power and enabling grace of the Lord.

Let us finish this chapter on a positive note: to be assured that if God has begun that good work in us, he will finish it. If we have really started the Christian race, we will arrive at the finishing line. Two verses from the hymn, *A debtor to mercy alone* clearly summarizes this wonderful theme.

The work which his goodness began,
The arm of his strength will complete;
His promise is Yea and Amen
And never was forfeited yet.
Things future, nor things that are now,
Not all things below nor above
Can make him his purpose forego
Or sever my soul from his love.

My name from the palms of his hands
Eternity will not erase;
Impressed on his heart it remains
In marks of indelible grace;
Yes, I to the end shall endure
As sure as the earnest is given;
More happy, but not more secure,
The glorified spirits in heaven.

Augustus Toplady (1740-78)

Homework

- 1. Give three Scripture references to show the impossibility of a true believer ever being lost.
- 2. How do we explain a situation where a person seems to have been converted and lived a Christian life for some time, but then turns away permanently?
- 3. How do we explain the warnings found in such passages as Hebrews 12:25?
- 4. Is perseverance promised or is it commanded? Explain your answer.
- 5. What means has God given to his people to enable them to persevere?
- 6. What practical effects should the doctrine of perseverance have on a believer?

10

God's Plan Complete – Glorification

When a runner finally crosses the finishing line of a marathon, there is a tremendous sense of relief. This is particularly so if he or she finishes first, but just to finish is relief enough. There were probably times when the runner had doubts about ever completing the course. Perhaps there were regrets because they had gone too fast or too slow in the early stages, but as the line is finally crossed there is a feeling of relief and joy despite the exhaustion.

As believers in the Lord Jesus Christ we never know exactly when we will finish our race. Death may come swiftly and unexpectedly. Even for the person who knows they are dying there is still some uncertainty. I heard of a man who was given only two weeks to live, yet he survived more than three months. The one thing certain is that either we shall die, or else the Lord Jesus Christ will come back. In the Christian race we are daily getting nearer to the finishing line.

Before we consider what happens as we cross that line, in death or at the return of Christ, it is helpful to take a look back at the ground covered so far. We have established that people, because of their sin and inability, cannot save themselves. Adam and Eve by their disobedience to God, plunged the whole human race into a state of depravity and enmity against God, and we have gladly followed in their rebellious footsteps. From that condition there can be no escape without divine intervention, but thanks be to God, he did intervene and planned and worked to redeem a people for himself. We might add that God did not begin to plan salvation after Adam and Eve sinned but before that happened. He was not caught by surprise by their disobedience, but had already anticipated it and provided for it. We were chosen in Christ '...before the creation of the world' (Eph. 1:4).

God's plan of redemption does not only involve saving sinful people, but rather a rescuing of the whole creation from the effects of sin. As we saw in the first chapter, the Fall had widespread repercussions: mankind became inherently sinful; they were separated from God; they had to endure hard work and sweat to gain their food; the ground began to bring forth thorns and thistles; childbirth became a painful process, and of course, death entered the human race. But the effects were even more far-reaching than that: the whole of creation was effected. We read that '...Even the heavens are not clean in his [God's] eyes' (Job 15:15). All this wrong and hurt God planned to put right. His ultimate purpose is well summed up in the following passage: 'And he made known to us the mystery of his will according to his good pleasure, which he purposed in Christ, to be put into effect when the times will have reached their fulfilment – to bring all things in heaven and on earth under one head, even Christ' (Eph. 1:9,10).

Everything will be under Christ's headship and will reflect Christ's glory. Glorification is a good word to describe this, and this is what we have to look forward to. At this point in time, if we are Christians, some of the effects of the Fall have been rectified – the guilt of our sin has been removed, and we are no longer separated from God. However, there is still much that has not yet been remedied: we still get sick and die; childbirth is still painful; we still find our gardens overrun with weeds, and obviously there is still a lot of sin in the world; even in our own lives. All this will be put to right in the future. When Peter was speaking to Jews about the Lord Jesus Christ, he said: 'He must remain in heaven until the time comes for God to restore everything' (Acts 3:21).

When will this happen?

In the verse just quoted from Acts 3, Peter indicated that the restoration would occur when Christ no longer remains in heaven: in other words at his second coming. Jesus Christ came into this world once when he was born at Bethlehem. That was an event that none who believe the Bible can dispute. But many times in the Bible we are told of an equally indisputable fact: that Christ will come a second time. The following three passages show this clearly. Jesus said:

- **1.** 'And if I go and prepare a place for you, I will come back and take you to be with me that you also may be where I am' (John 14:3).
- **2.** As the disciples watched Jesus ascending into heaven, the angels said to them: 'Men of Galilee…why do you stand here looking into the sky? This same Jesus, who has been taken from you into heaven, will come back in the same way you have seen him go into heaven' (Acts 1:11).
- **3.** In Hebrews we read: 'So Christ was sacrificed once to take away the sins of many people; and he will appear a second time, not to bear sin, but to bring salvation to those who are waiting for him' (Heb. 9:28).

Jesus will return in glory, visibly and bodily at some point in the future. Exactly when we do not know. We regularly hear of those who foolishly set dates for Christ's return, but they are always wrong because the time has not been revealed. Speaking about the time of his return, Jesus told the disciples: 'No one knows about the day or hour, not even the angels in heaven, nor the Son, but only the Father' (Matt. 24:36).

The return of Christ is an area of Christian doctrine over which there is much disagreement; but while the timetable surrounding his coming is disputed, no one who believes the Bible can deny that Jesus will return, and that following his second coming there will be the resurrection of all people, the judgement of all and the creation of a new heavens and a new earth. These events should not be merely academic to the believer, rather they should be anticipated with eagerness, just as the marathon runner eagerly anticipates the finishing line. It is easy to see how much Paul longed for that day when he wrote to the Philippians: 'But our citizenship is in heaven. And we eagerly await a Saviour from there, the Lord Jesus Christ, who, by the power that enables him to bring everything under his control, will transform our lowly bodies so that they will be like his glorious body' (Phil. 3:20,21).

What exactly then can we expect when Christ returns? A passage from Paul's letter to the Thessalonian church is helpful as a basis for our considerations: 'Brothers, we do not want you to be ignorant about those who fall asleep, or to grieve like the rest of men, who have no hope. We believe that Jesus died and rose again and so we believe that God will bring with Jesus those who have fallen asleep in him. According to the Lord's own word, we tell you that we who are still alive, who are left till the coming of the Lord, will certainly not precede those who have fallen asleep. For the Lord himself will come down from heaven, with a loud command, with the voice of the archangel and with the trumpet call of God, and the dead in Christ will rise first. After that, we who are alive and are left will be caught up together with them in the clouds to meet the Lord in the air. And so we will be with the Lord forever. Therefore encourage each other with these words' (1 Thess. 4:13-18).

Several points need to be noted:

First: there are two groups in view here; those who have died (fallen asleep) before Christ's return, and those still alive when he comes. The main reason for Paul writing as he did seemed to be that the people in the church at Thessalonica were concerned about those Christians who had died. They thought that in some way they were worse off than those still alive. Paul assures them that they are at no disadvantage.

Second: those who have died will be brought back with Christ when he returns. These will be disembodied spirits who have been in heaven since dying. The New Testament is clear that those believers who die go immediately into the presence of the Lord, even as Jesus told the dying thief: '…I tell you the truth, today you will be with me in paradise' (Luke 23:43). That is a blessed state – a sinless state, but it is not the final state, and we are not to anticipate this intermediate condition so much as the final resurrected state.

Third: Christ's return will be announced by a loud command, the voice of the archangel and a trumpet call. Elsewhere Paul speaks of '…the last trumpet…' (1 Cor. 15:52). Some refer to this as a secret coming, but the signs seem to indicate that it is very public, and an event of which all will be aware.

Fourth: the dead in Christ (those whose spirits come back with him), will be resurrected, their spirits being united with their new bodies. This will actually take place slightly ahead of the change in those still alive – '…The dead in Christ will rise first' (1 Thess. 4:16), thus confirming that they will be at no disadvantage.

Fifth: those believers who are still alive at that time will be caught up to meet the Lord in the air, their bodies being transformed to be like the bodies of those just resurrected. It might be helpful at this point to enquire about the nature of the resurrection body. Paul says it will be '…Like his [Christ's] glorious body' (Phil. 3:21). Assuming that our bodies will be like the body with which Jesus rose and appeared to the disciples, then it will be a physical body with flesh and bones (Luke 24:39). It will also be 'imperishable' and 'immortal' (1 Cor. 15:53), characterized by *'power'* and *'glory'* (1 Cor. 15:42). In a sense the new body is the first stage in our glorification. Adam and Eve were created with bodies, and as their sin brought about the corruption of the body as well as the soul, so the restoration of the creation will involve new bodies that can never die and never sin.

Sixth: from that time on all believers will be with the Lord forever. That is surely one of the most wonderful things about the future age – unbroken communion. Now we can enjoy times of close fellowship with our Saviour, but such seasons are all too infrequent, and often we have little or no sense of the Lord's presence. In glory we shall see him face to face. We shall be with him and be like him (1 John 3:2). Our fellowship with him will be never ending.

In chapter 4 of Thessalonians, Paul is focussing on the experience of the believer, but there is of course much more to consider. These verses speak of being caught up into the air: for never again will we set foot on the earth in its present condition. In conjunction with Christ's return is also the destruction of the earth as we know it. Peter writes: 'But the day of the Lord will come like a thief. The heavens will disappear with a roar; the elements will be destroyed by fire, and the earth and everything in it will be laid bare'... 'But in keeping with his promise we are looking forward to a new heaven and a new earth, the home of righteousness' (2 Peter 3:10,13).

Because the first earth has been polluted by the Fall, it will be renewed when Christ returns. There is some debate as to whether it will be a new earth or a renewed one. There seems to be an identity with the old earth, but clearly everything will be new. There is a parallel to the resurrection body. It will be new, yet with an identity to the old one – '...'It' is sown in dishonour, 'it' is raised in glory...' (1 Cor. 15:43).

The exact sequence of events is not spelled out here. Presumably the destruction of the old earth and the creation of the new will occur just after believers are raised up to be with Christ. Also to be fitted in is the judgement. John writes: 'Then I saw a great white throne and him who was seated on it. Earth and sky fled from his presence, and there was no place for them. And I saw the dead, great and small, standing before the throne, and books were opened. Another book was opened, which is the book of life. The dead were judged according to what they had done as recorded in the books. The sea gave up the dead that were in it, and death and Hades gave up the dead that were in them, and each person was judged according to what he had done. Then death and Hades were thrown into the lake of fire. The lake of fire is the second death. If anyone's name was not found written in the book of life, he was thrown into the lake of fire' (Rev. 20:11-15).

Note that at the time of the judgement, the earth and sky are said to have fled. This suggests that the judgement takes place in conjunction with the destruction of the old creation.

This is a general judgement, that is everyone, believers and unbelievers, stand together before the throne. Other Scriptures such as Matthew 25:31-46 confirm this.

The judgement is by works, again this is confirmed by other passages in the Bible – see John 5:28,29; Romans 2:7-10. This concept troubles some. If salvation is by grace not works, how can the judgement be by works? The works are not to determine whether or not people are saved, but to show that those who have true faith, demonstrate that faith by godly lives. In the Matthew 25 passage, although works are examined, the two groups are already separated into sheep and goats (verse 33). In the Revelation 20 passage, notice that there is a correspondence between those whose works are acceptable, and those whose names were written in the book of life, that is, the elect. This is a further confirmation that those whom God chose from eternity will all come to glory.

One other purpose of the judgement is to determine rewards

for believers. Passages such as the parable of the talents (Matt. 25:14-30) indicate that Christians will be rewarded for their faithfulness to the Lord, and as we differ greatly in our faithfulness and level of holiness, it is appropriate that rewards should differ also. John says: 'Watch out that you do not lose what you have worked for, but that you may be rewarded fully' (2 John 8).

In our studies we are considering primarily the fate of believers. They will be resurrected, judged by their works, rewarded and live forever in the presence of the Lord. It may be appropriate at this point to mention that unbelievers will also be resurrected, judged and cast into hell forever. The period of the punishment of the ungodly is co-extensive with the bliss of the righteous. At the close of the description of the judgement of the sheep and goats, Jesus told his disciples, speaking first of the wicked: 'Then they will go away to eternal punishment, but the righteous to eternal life' (Matt. 25:46). While as Christians we can rejoice at the prospect of glory, it is good to remember that there are multitudes who cannot look forward to eternal happiness, and we need to be concerned for their souls, seeking to bring the gospel to them.

One other thing that can be brought in here is the defeat of Satan. The downfall of Adam and Eve came about because of Satan's temptation. From that time on there has been a constant warfare between Satan and the human race – the offspring of the woman (Gen. 3:15). While some measure of punishment was inflicted on Satan at the time of the Fall (Gen. 3:14,15), and a further judgement added at the time of Christ – '…now the prince of this world will be driven out' (John 12:31), his ultimate punishment is reserved for the final judgement when he will be cast into the '…lake of burning sulphur…' (Rev. 20:10).

Following the judgement, God's people will live upon the new earth. Most of us tend to speak about heaven as our future home, but strictly that is only the abode of believers between death and the resurrection. Following the events we have described, our eternal dwelling place will be on earth. Listen to John's words as he describes the scene following the judgement: 'Then I saw a new heaven and a new earth, for the first heaven and the first earth had passed away, and there was no longer any sea. I saw the Holy City, the New Jerusalem, coming down out of heaven from God, prepared as a bride beautifully dressed for her husband. And I heard a loud voice from the throne saying, "Now the dwelling of God is with men, and he will live with them. They will be his people, and God himself will be with them and be their God. He will wipe every tear from their eyes. There will be no more death or mourning or crying or pain, for the old order of things has passed away"'... (Rev. 21:1-4).

The church here is described under two figures: a city and a bride; both familiar pictures of God's people in the Old and New Testaments (Isa. 52:1-10; 62:5; Heb. 11:10; 2 Cor. 11:2; Rev. 19:7). A city suggests order and security: a bride suggests a love relationship. The church descends from heaven, presumably to the earth. It is common to think of the New Jerusalem, described in Revelation 21 and 22, as the place where the church will live, but the New Jerusalem 'is' the church, the bride of Christ.

Because the world to come is presented to us in figurative terms, it is hard to get a clear concept of what it will be like. I suppose we can say that as it is described figuratively, it means that we cannot grasp the glory of that future age from our present perspective. Also, because so little detail is given, it means that we do not need to know more than is revealed, and therefore it is pointless to speculate about things like whether there will be animals in glory or whether we shall eat and drink there. What can we say about the world to come?

It will be a place of unspeakable glory. We are told that in the New Jerusalem there will be no temple and no sun or moon.

The reason being that '...The Lord God Almighty and the Lamb are its temple' and, '...The glory of God gives it light, and the Lamb is its lamp' (Rev. 21:22,23). In the new age everything will be Christ-centred. We shall be with him and enjoy his fellowship. Nothing will mar our enjoyment of him, and nothing will detract from his glory.

It will be a place of eternal comfort. As we read in the passage quoted above, there will be no more death, no mourning, no crying and no pain. There will be nothing to mar our happiness; nothing to spoil our enjoyment of that wonderful realm.

A question sometimes asked in connection with this is, 'How could I enjoy the world to come if I knew that my loved one was in hell?' That is not an easy one to answer. All we can say is that we shall see things then from a different perspective. Obviously hell will not spoil God's enjoyment of eternity. Many whom he created will be suffering eternal torment, but their punishment will glorify his justice. It may be hard for us to grasp the concept now, but if there is no crying or mourning in heaven, then we must accept by faith that in that day we shall see things as God sees them.

It will be a place of everlasting righteousness. There will be no sin in heaven. 'Nothing impure will ever enter it...' (Rev. 21:27). Now we have to bemoan our sin and often confess that we have dishonoured God. In glory that will never happen. Imagine going through even one day without having to confess our sins! In the New Jerusalem that will be true day after day – if there are separate days – '...There will be no night there' (verse 25). The righteousness that we will have will not simply be by obedience to God's laws, but by conformity to Jesus Christ. We shall be like him.

It will be a place of useful service. We read that '...His [God's] servants will serve him' (Rev. 22:3). The picture that some have painted of glory is of saints floating on clouds playing harps, or of a vast choir singing unceasingly. Neither of these are accurate pictures of what is portrayed in the Bible. Doubtless we shall spend all our time praising God, but praise is not only that which is uttered by mouth. In the world to come every activity will bring glory to God and the Lamb. We shall be involved in serving God. Exactly how is not revealed, but the parable of the minas (Luke 19:11-27) suggests that the rewards given to believers are not material goods but responsibilities. This is in keeping with the stated fact that we shall reign with Christ (2 Tim. 2:12; Rev. 5:10). In the Garden of Eden Adam and Eve were not swinging in hammocks all day long, they were involved in tending the garden. The new earth will not be a place of inactivity but of useful and productive service.

In our considerations then we have arrived at the finishing line, and seen something of the conclusion of God's plan of salvation. All of the effects of the Fall will then be remedied. Sin will be cleansed from the creation: Satan will be damned: death will be banished: the curse will be lifted: there will be no thorns or thistles in the new earth; and of course there will be no pain in childbirth for all pain will be gone. Further than that, there will be no reproduction in glory (Matt. 22:30).

Yes, God saves sinners. God alone can save them. It is a task far beyond the capabilities of any human being. God can and he does save them. He doesn't improve them or help them to improve themselves, he saves them, he transforms them and makes them like Jesus Christ. When we believe, he saves us from the guilt and penalty of sin: throughout our earthly life he saves us progressively from the power of sin, and at the resurrection he will save us from every trace of sin. God saves sinners – *not* the righteous, for there are no righteous people by nature. He saves those who had rebelled against him: those who did not seek him until he first sought them: those who would never have come to him had he not drawn them by an irresistible love. It is all of God's doing: all of grace. At last a

Thirsting Soul has found true refreshment. To him be the praise and the glory!

How vast the benefits divine,
Which we in Christ possess!
We're saved from guilt and every sin
And called to holiness.

It's not for works which we have done,
Or shall hereafter do,
But he of his abounding love
Salvation does bestow.

The glory, Lord, from first to last,
Is due to thee alone;
Aught to ourselves we dare not take
Or rob thee of thy crown.

Our glorious Surety undertook
Redemption's wondrous plan;
And grace was given us in him
Before the world began.

Not one of all the chosen race,
But shall to heaven attain:
Partake on earth the purposed grace
And then with Jesus reign.

Augustus Toplady (1740-78)

Homework

- 1. List the effects of the Fall of man and show how all these are remedied by the work of Christ.
- 2. How would you answer someone who said that Christ's return had already taken place?
- 3. What happens now when a believer dies?
- 4. What will happen to those Christians who have already died when Christ returns?
- 5. What will happen to those believers still alive when Christ returns?
- 6. If salvation is by grace, why will believers have to stand before the judgement?
- 7. List as many contrasts as you can between life on this earth and life on the new earth.

11

Epilogue

In Ecclesiastes 12:13 , the writer says, 'Now all has been heard;...' Doubtless many more things could have been said with profit in this book, but all that the author intended to say has been said. However, I cannot lay down my pen (as older writers would have said) – in reality, quit my keyboard, without a word of challenge to the reader.

We have traced God's plan of salvation from start to finish. We have seen our own sinful state that necessitated God's plan to save sinners. We have seen his electing grace in choosing some to be saved. We have looked at the work of Jesus Christ to redeem God's elect by his all-sufficient atonement. We have considered God's gracious calling of sinners to himself by the Holy Spirit. Then we saw how people are brought to the knowledge of God in repentance and faith. We saw the rich blessing given to those who believe – they are justified and brought into God's family. Next we traced how God sanctifies his people and causes them to persevere to the end. And what a wonderful end it will be as all God's people are brought to the unspeakable glories of heaven and the new earth. They will see Jesus face to face; they will be like him, and they will spend all eternity in his presence. The great question remains – what is our response to these great truths?

Doubtless most of those who have read these pages will be believers. How do you respond, Christian friend? How do we who have been saved by God's wonderful grace respond to a consideration of that grace? Surely we should be filled with amazement to think that the God of heaven, the one who made the universe, should ever set his love upon us! We ought to be humbled to realize that the Lord saved us when we neither deserved nor sought his salvation. We should be filled with praise when we consider all the blessings that are ours in Jesus Christ. We are 'blessed …in the heavenly realms with every spiritual blessing in Christ' (Eph1:3).

However our response should be more than just praise – important and necessary as that is; we should be so filled with gratitude to the Lord that we want more than anything else to please and obey him. There are times when all of us struggle in the Christian life. We find it hard to do what we know to be right. But if we contemplate what the Lord Jesus Christ has suffered for us, we should be filled with shame at our reluctance to obey him, and feel a great desire to please him who has loved us and redeemed us. All of the truths we have considered together in this book should spur us on to follow Christ and be more like him.

But are there some who read these pages who have not experienced the salvation described here? Perhaps you have never yet realized the greatness of your sin against God and you have never repented of those sins and turned to the Lord. You may read about the atonement with some degree of intellectual understanding, but do you know what it is to have your sins forgiven? You have read about justification, but do you know that you are right with God? You have read the chapter on adoption, but can you sincerely and with a loving heart address God as your Father? You have come to the last chapter and enjoyed reading about the glories of heaven and the world to come. You have seen something of the blessedness and joy of those who will be there, but are you certain that you will be there, enjoying the presence of the Lord forever? There is a terrible danger that people can read with interest about the Lord's salvation without ever experiencing it. And so I urge you to be sure that you are one of God's people, not by trying to pry into the eternal counsels of God to see whether you are elect (something we can never do), but by believing in Christ. Remember the message that Paul preached wherever he went: 'First to those in Damascus, then to those in Jerusalem and in all Judea, and to the Gentiles also, I preached that they should repent and turn to God and prove their repentance by their deeds' (Acts 26:20).

The way to be right with God is by repentance and faith. You must see your sin and how offensive it is to God. Then you must confess your sin and turn to Christ. He has died for sinners. His shed blood is sufficient to cleanse the worst of sinners. Cry out to him for pardon. Ask him to have mercy on you, and he will. If you call upon him, he promises to save you (Acts 2:21). If you come to him in repentance and faith, he will receive you. (John 6:37). If you confess your sins he will forgive you (1 John 1:9). May God grant that you will not put this book down until you have experienced personally the salvation about which you have read. Yes, God saves sinners, and he will save you if you seek him with all your heart.